JUNG'S THREE THEORIES OF RELIGIOUS EXPERIENCE

JUNG'S THREE THEORIES OF RELIGIOUS EXPERIENCE

J. Harley Chapman

Studies in the Psychology of Religion
Volume 3

The Edwin Mellen Press
Lewiston/Queenston

Library of Congress Cataloging-in-Publication Data

Chapman, J. Harley, 1940-
    Jung's three theories of religious experience.

    (Studies in the psychology of religion ; v. 3)
    Bibliography: p.
    Includes index.
    1. Experience (Religion)--History of doctrines--
20th century. 2. Jung, C. G. (Carl Gustav), 1875-1961--
Contributions in theory of religious experience.
I. Title. II. Title: Jung's 3 theories of religious
experience. III. Series.
BL53.C42 1988   291.4'2   87-20465
ISBN 0-88946-245-3

This is volume 3 in the continuing series
Studies in the Psychology of Religion
Volume 3 ISBN 0-88946-245-3
SPR Series ISBN 0-88946-247-X

The Edwin Mellen Press   The Edwin Mellen Press
Box 450   Box 67
Lewiston, New York   Queenston, Ontario
USA 14092   L0S 1L0 CANADA

Printed in the United States of America

To
Jean Berglof Chapman
necessarily
gratefully

TABLE OF CONTENTS

ACKNOWLEDGEMENTS

This work owes much to many: initially to mentors Langdon Gilkey, Peter Homans, and David Tracy for patient guidance and thoughtful criticism of my ideas; to colleagues Jerome Stone and Stephen Franklin for intellectual stimulation and support; to June Singer for counsel and encouragement; to two former students, now friends, Charles Woods and Sally Leighton, for their active interest throughout; and then to concerned friends and colleagues too numerous to mention individually but nonetheless deeply appreciated. Martin Ryan, Dean of Liberal Arts at William Rainey Harper College, has been unfailingly helpful, and the manuscript has been expertly prepared by Lisa Larsen, Alan Jeude, Benjamin Buckley, Joan Drake, Lawrence J. Haffner, and Mary Frances Burns, who very competently prepared the index. My sons John, Sam, and Mike have borne without complaint the frustration of having me preoccupied with "the project." Most importantly of all, Jean Berglof Chapman, my wife, has supported me caringly through it all, and it is to her that I dedicate this work.

JUNG'S THREE THEORIES OF RELIGIOUS EXPERIENCE

CHAPTER ONE
JUNG'S UNDERSTANDING OF RELIGIOUS EXPERIENCE:
AN INTRODUCTION

In the following essay I attempt an elucidation of C. G. Jung's understanding of religious experience, specifically, how Jung in fact explains this pervasive and important human phenomenon. I assume at the outset that anything of general importance, attested by the experiences of men and women across space and through time, is worthy of the best human attempts at understanding. That we live today in an increasingly desacralized world does not alter the fact of the importance of religious experience or even of its existence. That something is problematic is more a matter of how it is rather than what or whether it is. Furthermore, the problematicity of religious experience, at least for the critically reflective and culturally sensitive, leads to a second concern: justification. Religious experience cries out for explanation (the best explanation, we might argue, providing justification) since by itself religious experience does not account for itself, depending rather on one or several schemata for elucidation. Religious experience is ambiguous at best, and out of its internal richness it can and does generate alternative accountings: some rooted in socio-cultural dynamics; some in the psychological vicissitudes of individuals; some in the aesthetic, moral, noetic, and ontological dimensions of experience. I take it that a variety of explanations advanced from various cultural disciplines is a cognitive enrichment, not an impoverishment; methodological totalitarianism is in every case to be abominated.

Theories explain; they do not essentially describe or interpret. Infinite and nuanced descriptions of particulars never account for why things are as they are and not otherwise; there is a logical difference between the two. Neither does interpretation coincide with explanation since the former requires an interpreter who is grasped sufficiently enough by a symbolic content to be a bearer of its meaning into a different context.[1] By contrast, an explanation essentially accounts for the "the necessity in the data," for why things can be expected to occur in certain ways, or, if the explanation is more theoretical and less empirical, why certain categories organized in hierarchical relationships better account for what is known than other alternatives open to one. Again, while interpretation and explanation can overlap in human discourse, the functions are logically distinct. The concern in this essay is with explanation.

Specifically, however, it is the work of C. G. Jung that is the lode for our mining. He is an important, if controversial, shaper of twentieth-century thought, standing along with Freud as one of the great pioneers of depth psychology. More suggestive than exhaustive, Jung's thought is remarkably wide-ranging and his influence on a number of disciplines--psychology, education, ethology, literary criticism, comparative religion, and theology, to name a few--is unmistakable. Yet here our focus is on Jung's understanding of religious experience: its nature, ground, and consequences. I am not concerned with providing a Jungian interpretation of individual life or cultural phenomena. That is a hermeneutic task for those interested in such. My concern is with explaining religious experience, and I turn to Jung as a possible fruitful source. This essay should be of some interest to two main groups of readers: (1) critical investigators and assessors of religious experience-- social scientists, phenomenologists and philosophers of religion, and theologians; and (2) Jung scholars and others interested in analytical and archetypal psychology who wish to comprehend how Jung in fact understands religious experience, or ought to do so in light of his theoretical commitments.

The Thesis, Broadly Stated

I claim that Jung in fact does not have one theory of religious experience, but three. I shall argue this by elaborating in some detail what I understand to be three different but related theories. While adumbrated here and there throughout Jung's writings, none of these three is explicitly or completely spelled out.[2] The three theories, which I shall call the scientific-psychological, the phenomenological-mythological, and the metaphysical-theological, are each jointly determined by (a) the varying explanatory intent, (b) the shift in meaning of key terms, and (c) the employment of different models.

With respect to the varying explanatory intent: (i) if Jung is engaging in science, there is implied a

particular understanding of the goal (knowledge of
nature), of the activity (critical inquiry,
investigation), of the attitude (objective, self-
eliminating), of the subject (observational-
intellectual inquirer, only a partial self), and of
the object (god-image); (ii) if Jung is engaging in
phenomenology, there is suggested an understanding of
the goal (becoming an individual, a whole), of the
activity (careful consideration of numina, dialogue
with the presented other), of the attitude
(subjective, self-involving), of the subject (totally
engaged "becomer"), and of the object (archetype of
the self or _imago dei_); (iii) if Jung is engaging in
metaphysics or theology, there is indicated yet
another understanding of the goal (understanding of,
and relatedness to, the Infinite), of the activity
(ontological reflection, "confession"), of the
attitude (trans-subjective, abandoning), of the
subject (realizer-confessor), and of the object (God,
The Ultimate). As theory, each necessarily attempts
to explain something. The explanandum is in each case
"empirical," and the explanans "theoretical." In the
first theory, the empirical is the observational, and
the theoretical is a scientific hypothesis; in the
second theory, the empirical is the experiential, and
the theoretical a myth;[3] and in the third, the
empirical is the existential, and the theoretical a
metaphysical or ontological theory.

With respect to the shift in meaning of key
terms, Jung understands, for example, "archetype" to
mean in some contexts an unobserved, unexperienced,
and unexperienceable theoretical entity; in others, a
dynamic form-meaning radiating in an image, hence
experienceable, as well as a dynamic agency having

intentionality, hence personal; in yet others, an[4] attribute of the Creator or metaphysical ultimate. Likewise, "consciousness" according to the context can mean a noetic act, an ethical act, or a metaphysical attribute.[5] "Psyche" has manifold nuances; various aspects are highlighted, some in this context, some in that.[6] The term "experience of God" shifts from a largely descriptive term to a largely explanatory term.[7] The list can be extended.

With respect to the models employed, Jung[8] understands the psyche as a <u>stream</u> (of vital energy),[9] a <u>quest</u> (for wholeness), and a <u>creature</u> or <u>splinter</u> ("of the infinite deity").[10] Jung's well-known distinction between the individual psyche and the collective psyche is comprehended by and is internal to each of the models. These models are elaborated in varying ways and given more or less formal treatment. In post-positivistic philosophy of science it is increasingly seen that all theories are rooted in images and that even the meaning of theoretical terms is derived from the model, not from observation.[11]

How Jung Can Fruitfully Be Read

The claim that three different theories of religious experience rooted in three different models of the psyche are to be found in Jung determines the hermeneutic to be employed. Arguably, all theoretical activity is rooted in various imaginative graspings of selected aspects of the behavior of phenomena and of systems of phenomena. The image, if not the symbol, gives rise indeed to thought. It is important, therefore, to intuit the image in each of the theories Jung is employing. Sensing and clarifying the underlying image as a model has the virtue of avoiding the dangers of two standard approaches to Jung's thought. First, it rejects the easily adopted, ahistorical reading of Jung in which everything in the Collected Works, at least from 1920 onward, is to be understood as an element in a system of psychological ideas. While this approach is based on the continuity of intention which more often than not marks a creative mind, it staticizes living thought and encourages a fundamentalistic hermeneutic.[12] Secondly, it demurs at an evolutionary-developmental approach in which the later is always understood to be an advance over the earlier, and that with the later Jung repudiates the earlier. This approach allows for dynamic thinking and intellectual growth but distorts the perduring elements in a thinker's corpus.[13] It seems far preferable, at least for the purposes of the study of religious experience, which is a pervasive concern in Jung's thinking, to sort out the models he used, which, while distinct in themselves, are often interwoven in such a way that Jung's real intent is obscured. Sorted out, each model is seen to have an exemplary instantiation at a particular period of Jung's career. A model is relatively more enduring than an image;[14] and thus while exemplarily instantiated at a particular period, it is seen as present or recurring over a span of years and perhaps throughout his career. Consequently, while we find the stream model primarily exemplified between 1912 and 1928, we find Jung animadverting to this model of the psyche and the energetic theory built thereon in his Memories, Dreams, Reflections (the relevant section written in 1959), nearly a half century after his first use of it. Furthermore, the model of the psyche as a quest for wholeness, primarily instanced between roughly 1930 and the middle 1950's, is foreshadowed in his doctoral dissertation (1902) and[15] continues up until his last published letter (1961). Finally, the splinter-creature model, primarily evident in Jung's last decade, is evinced in his concern with the Infinite and the individual's relatedness to it, a concern not confined to "Late Thoughts,"[16] when his scientific labors had ended, and when one in advanced age is allowed musings of a transcendental sort. Rather, his autobiography shows an early and precocious interest in metaphysical questions, and his early religious experiences were determinative for his development and relationships. Furthermore, his 1916 references to "the eternal and infinite" (das ewige und unendliches) and the pleroma (das Pleroma)[17] are of a piece with the references to the Infinite (Das Grenzenlose, Das Unendliches) of 1959.[18] Moreover, Jung's mid-career reference (1938) to the pervasion of the Boundless (Das Grenzenlose) by psychic laws[19] testifies to Jung's career-long assumption of the warrantability of asserting a trans-psychic ground. For Jung, foreground implies a background, and the science of psychology, while a legitimately limited enterprise, is not metaphysically groundless. The psyche, whatever else may be said of it scientifically, is also a "creature" or "splinter," an attribute or aspect of the metaphysical ultimate.

There are three discernible models although there are modifications possible within each. For example, as I shall point out in the next chapter, while Jung speaks of the psyche as a stream of vital energy (theoretically formalized as a teleologically ordered, relatively closed energy system), his treatment of it in late career (1947) as compared with an early expression (1912) shows some significant changes. However, these are changes <u>within</u> the basic image, not from it to another.

Reading Jung, therefore, in terms of basic models and the theories of religious experience they legitimate allows for a nuanced interpretation that gives room for the various activities in which Jung was engaged--science, phenomenology, and metaphysics. Furthermore, it allows a positive, non-reductive interpretation of Jung's contributions and makes possible a discerning response to his thought. While this is by no means the only way to read Jung, it is a fruitful, hence good, one. We turn now to this task.

1
    I draw here on Leander E. Keck, "Toward a Theology of Rhetoric/Preaching," in Practical Theology: The Emerging Field in Theology Church, and World, ed. Don Browning (New York: Harper and Row, 1983), p. 134.
    2
    That a theory is inexplicit does not entail its absence. Needless to say, sensitivity, caution, and fair-mindedness are desired virtues of any interpretation, especially when one is engaging in some sort of "source criticism," as my argument requires that I do. If there is a persisting attempt to explain, usually signaled by the presence of some technical vocabulary, then I take it that a theory is more or less in view. Furthermore, that a theory is incomplete is no argument against it as a theory since most, if not all, theories in the natural and social sciences, the generally accepted domain of theory, are incomplete since the relations among the elements of any theory are often imprecisely spelled out. See Garvin McCain and Erwin M. Segal, The Game of Science, 3rd ed. (Monterey, California: Brooks/Cole Publishing Co., 1977), p. 99.
    3
    Whatever else myths do--orient toward mystery, evoke certain attitudes, enjoin some behaviors and proscribe others, entertain, etc.--they explain. They attempt to say why certain events occur(red). Though neither metaphysics nor science, myths are theoretical in that they redescribe certain experiences in other terms and in other presuppositional contexts. The shift from everyday presuppositions to those of an imaginal (not imaginary) world betokens a shift from the empirical to the theoretical. A man condemned as a criminal and cruelly executed is reinterpreted as the son of a heavenly god, sent to earth on a particular mission of loving sacrifice which when completed is returned, vindicated, to the place of honor at the god's right hand. Such an imagined world has its own presuppositions--what can and cannot happen--generalizations, laws, predictive possibili- ties, and tests. Like all explanation, it has reference to and attempts to explain some empirical matter; and, like all explanations, it goes beyond the empirical facts. That an explanation is "fantastic" does not count against it as an explanation. The notion that a theoretical explanation requires a shift in the context of presuppostions is drawn from Paul Snyder, Toward One Science (New York: St. Martins

Press, Inc., 1978), p. 98.

4

For the notion of the irrepresentable, unexperienceable archetype, see, inter alia, Jung, CW 8:213 and CW 9/i:79; for the archetype as an experienceable form-meaning endowed with subjectivity, see Jung, CW 8:214, CW 11:469, and CW 17:110; for the notion of the archetype as an attribute of the Creator, see Jung to W. Niederer, 1 October 1953, Letters, 2:130. Unless otherwise indicated, references to Jung's writings will be as follows:

C. G. Jung, The Collected Works of C. G. Jung, eds. Sir Herbert Read, Michael Fordham, and Gerhard Adler, Bollingen Series 20, trans. R.F.C. Hull (except vol. 6) (Princeton: Princeton University Press, 1961-1976). All references to Jung's Collected Works hereafter will be by volume and page number, as CW 8:213.

C. G. Jung, Memories, Dreams, Reflections, recorded and edited by Aniela Jaffé, trs. Richard and Clara Winston (New York: Random House, Vintage Books, 1963). Hereafter MDR.

C. G. Jung, Letters, eds. Gerhard Adler and Aniela Jaffe, trans. R. F. C. Hull, Bollingen Series 95, 2 vols. (Princeton: Princeton University Press, 1975). Hereafter abbreviated Letters, followed by volume and page number, as in Letters 2:130.

5

For consciousness as a noetic act see Jung, CW 8:171, and MDR, p. 322; for consciousness as an ethical act see Jung, CW 8:210, 361, CW 11: 158n.9; for consciousness as a metaphysical attribute see Jung to Anonymous, 2 January 1957, Letters, 2:342.

6

For various nuances of "psyche" see Jung, CW 6:465ff., and CW 8:139.

7

I argue this at length in Chapters Two, Three, and Four below.

8

The notion of the psyche as a stream is to be found inter alia in Jung's essay : "On Psychic Energy" in CW 8:37, 38. This model will be elaborated in Chapter Two below.

9

The notion of a quest for wholeness is implicit in Jung's understanding of the individuation process, which on a human level is achieved only through intentional action, whether conscious or unconscious. Among the numerous references possible see CW 9/i:275, CW 7:173, CW 8:226, CW 18:285, 289, and CW 13:300.

10

    The phrase "splinter of the infinite deity" is found in Jung's MDR, p. 4. Jung also uses the term "creature" in various places: see ibid., p. 333. As I will point out in Chapter Four below, there is an ambiguity latent in Jung's notion of creation. Whether Jung has a satisfactory doctrine of creation is doubtful; his use of the term "creature" seems to be sanctioned more by tradition than by the logic of his position. However, for the present, the ambiguity will be allowed to stand.

11

    I am indebted here to Ian Barbour's understanding of models. See particularly his Myths, Models, and Paradigms (New York: Harper & Row, Publishers, 1974), p. 40.

12

    The natural drive toward seeing systematic coherence in a thinker's work bedevils Jung's interpreters of all stripes--orthodox disciples, pedagogical systematizers, and unsympathetic critics. For an over-systematic presentation by a loyal interpreter, see Jolande Jacobi, The Psychology of C. G. Jung, tr. Ralph Manheim (New Haven: Yale University Press, 1968), where the author speaks, for example, of Jung's "system" (p. 2). For a just critique of such tendency see Naomi R. Goldenberg, "Jung After Feminism," in Beyond Androcentrism, ed. Rita M. Gross (Missoula, Montana: Scholars Press, 1977), p. 56. A sample of an over-organized presentation of Jung's ideas by sympathetic academic psychologists is Calvin S. Hall and Vernon J. Nordby, A Primer of Jungian Psychology (New York: American Library, 1973). For a systematic but unfriendly criticism see Edward Glover, Freud or Jung? (New York: World Publishing Co., 1965).

13

    The developmental approach is less often attempted in Jungian studies, the most explicit of which, however, at least as regards the psychology of religion, is Raymond Hostie, S.J., Religion and the Psychology of Jung, tr. G. R. Lamb (New York: Sheed and Ward, 1957). For all its promise Hostie's work is ultimately flawed through inaccuracies and lack of sympathy. A more helpful and nuanced treatment is the diachronic approach of James W. Heisig, Imago Dei: A Study of C. G. Jung's Psychology of Religion (Lewisburg, Penn.: Bucknell University Press, 1979). About his procedure Heisig writes: "Although the approach is chronological the task is a demanding one, since no aspect of Jung's thought shows a clear

process of evolution [author's emphasis]. Indeed, the
temporal model to describe the unfolding of Jung's
ideas may be a restraining bias that conceals as much
as it discloses." p. 10.
    14
    This has been suggested by Barbour's "a metaphor
is used only momentarily, whereas a model is used in a
sustained and systematic fashion" in ibid., p. 16.
    15
    Jung to John A. Sanford, 10 March 1961, <u>Letters</u>,
2:360.
    16
    Jung, MDR, Ch. XII.
    17
    Ibid., p. 379.
    18
    Ibid., p. 325.
    19
    Jung, CW 11:105.

CHAPTER TWO
THE SCIENTIFIC-PSYCHOLOGICAL THEORY
OF RELIGIOUS EXPERIENCE

The first theory to be discussed is Jung's scientific-psychological theory of religious experience, by which is meant that religious experience is to be understood or explained in terms of the methodological assumptions and procedures of the scientific study of the psyche. While Jung claims that most of what he wrote for public perusal was scientific--he explicitly disclaimed only Answer to Job,[1] and under the pressure of debate with Martin Buber he characterized his privately published Septem Sermones ad Mortuum as a "poem"[2]--the claim advanced here is that this scientific-psychological theory of religious experience has its primary positioning in three texts: Psychology of the Unconscious (1912);[3] "The Theory of Psycho-Analysis," a lecture series given in 1912 at Fordham University; and the essay "On Psychic Energy" (1928).[4] The first two will be considered together since they were written within the same period (1911-1912), since there seems to be no significant differences in theoretical understanding, and since the second and more didactic piece helps to clarify and stabilize the welter of brilliant but chaotically presented insights of the first.[5] The third will then be presented as the other half of the arch, concluding a line of thought which began in the

first. The first part of the present chapter will
treat the early formulation ("The Theory: A First
Sketch"); the second, the later ("The Theory
Reconsidered and Rounded Out"). I will also avail
myself of scattered insights throughout Jung's
writings and letters as they buttress and flesh out
the theory.

The Theory: A First Sketch

In 1911 and 1912 Jung published Wandlungen und
Symbole der Libido, which was translated into English
in 1916 as Psychology of the Unconscious, bearing two
subtitles: A Study of the Transformations and
Symbolisms of the Libido and A Contribution to the
History of the Evolution of Thought. The English
title and subtitles are all attempts to express the
theme and intentions of this many-sided and brilliant,
even if confusing, work. In it Jung begins to assert
his intellectual independence of Freud, though at best
it is a transitional work of a psychoanalyst on the
way to becoming an analytical psychologist; Jung's
past and present conflict with his future in the form
of insights and intuitions as yet unassimilated. As a
psychoanalyst he attempts to work within the confines
of the theory of wish-fulfillment and an extraverted
viewpoint; as an analytical psychologist in the making
he understands libido in a neutral sense as psychic
energy and searches culture history for clues to
understand the processes of individual transformation.
For the first time Jung opens the door to what will
remain a life-long passion and a hallmark of his
thought: the focus on mythology and religion. While
in later years he was to repudiate some of his claims
and attitudes and in the leisure of old age was to

revise the book substantially, many of the emphases, expressions, and orientations were to remain constant.[6] I argue that this major work, while admittedly a first treatment, is crucial for understanding much of Jung's later work, for here he laid down the lines of his development.

Activity and Assumptions of the Science of Psychology

Whatever Jung will have to say about religious experience in this work will be set in the context of his work as a scientist, in particular as a psychologist; consequently, we must explore how he understood the activity and assumptions of the psychologist and the nature and function of the psyche as psychology revealed it to be.

As a scientist, an identity in which Jung took a life-long pride, he sought understanding of empirical processes. This was a self-conscious turning away from a dogmatic, non-empirical attempt at knowing, which he saw both traditional religion and philosophy as making. Thus, he repudiated belief and transcendent speculation as illegitimate.[7] Whether or not he was fair in his treatment of both religion and philosophy, his rejection of what he saw as non-empirical and dogmatic served to underline his own intention to be and to be identified as a scientist.

One consequence of this stance was a tendency toward positivism. While he took pains to say that psychology was neutral with respect to any transcendentalism[8] (presumably, he means any and all forms of religion and philosophy which assume a non-empirical principle or reality), it is clear that for any significant purpose an espousal of transcendent

reality was impossible. Again and again, pressed by
critics who claimed that he was engaging in
metaphysics, Jung adopted as a defense a quasi-
nominalist and positivist position: the unconscious
was "a mere term" and not to be understand as an ens
per se.[9] Methodologically, Jung disposed of any
temptation toward transcendentalizing by incorporating
metaphysics, both rational-speculative and
confessional (theology), within psychology:
metaphysics is nothing more than metapsychology, and
metapsychology is nothing more than a self-reflective
attempt at understanding.[10] Seemingly, Jung is not
curious about the meta-empirical status of scientific
statements (are they only empirical generalizations?
are they synthetic a priori judgments? do they intend
the structures of reality? are they possibly objec-
tively true?). He seems to be content to say that
metaphysical statements are judgments made by human
personalities, which personalities can now be
understood by the new science of psychoanalysis. His
cosmology, what kinds of things there are in reality,
seems to be, from a static viewpoint, roughly
Cartesian: there are physical phenomena (what he calls
"reality") and psychological phenomena. This is
apparent particularly in human beings, which possess
an intellectual and an animal nature. Dynamically
considered, Jung's view is a species of emergent
evolutionism, if not an evolutionary epiphenomenalism,
in that psyche is a development of the biological
organism, which has its mysterious origins in the
material substance of the universe.

Whether one ultimately is to take Jung's
positivism at this stage--and beyond--as simply
methodological or in fact substantive is difficult to

assess. It is the case that Kant had a powerful effect on Jung from his university days on; and it may be assumed that Jung, following Kant, held out the possibility of a metaphysics of a tempered sort. However, Jung in effect, as noted earlier, has already translated into psychological reality whatever could be claimed by metaphysicians to be real.[11]

Science for Jung is necessarily reductionistic. It reduces effects to their causes, phenomena to temporary energy states (in psychology symbols are reducible to "libido psychic energy and its fixed primitive qualities"),[12] the many expressions to the one principle. In Jung's case, mythological products are translatable (and should be so translated) into psychological ones, from which they originally sprang.[13]

Whether or not Jung believed that a scientific reduction without remainder of religious imagery and statement to be possible is an interesting question. Despite his seeming confidence in the power of psychoanalysis to explain religious and mythological language, he gives some evidence that he realizes that science cannot dispense with myth and that the mythology of a people is not simply the magnification of individual psychological processes. Jung speaks of the beauty of the myth,[14] and a myth containing such value ought to be retained if properly understood. Thus, myth possesses some value not reducible to knowledge. It seems to be the case that human beings are attracted to myths before and after psychoanalysis, during which process one presumably attains to an understanding of one's psychodynamics. The myth possesses some value which lures the mind and feelings in a way that case histories do not; the psychoanalyst Jung, fascinated by mythology, is his own evidence.

Science is based on generalities, uniformities, the self-identical (uniformity over time), and the universally valid.[15] This would seem to make problematic the status of a psychology that deals with the irreducibly unique human personality. For this reason Jung averred that the individual consciousness made "the most unfavorable object imaginable for psychology" since it obscures the "overwhelmingly clear and therefore universally obtrusive general facts upon which a science must be founded."[16] The non-individual but clearly observable general facts about human personality are elements of the unconscious psyche. The true object, therefore, of any non-psychophysical psychology is the unconscious. Jung was subsequently to make this a central affirmation.

A science (knowledge) of the unconscious (unknown psyche) is peculiar, even paradoxical, and was seen to be even more so in the early decades of this century. To make this position understandable Jung opened his book with an essay entitled "Concerning the Two Kinds of Thinking," in which he distinguished directed thinking from dream or fantasy thinking. Of directed thinking, on the one hand, he claimed that its goal was to communicate with the environment through speech and language, adapting to, imitating, and acting upon (external) reality; it was conscious throughout, took effort and was exhausting to the thinker; it took as its source as well as its ultimate aim the objective world; it was more or less a modern achievement, modern science being its exemplar, though medieval scholasticism, despite its preoccupation with fantasy objects, was a precursor.

Dream or fantasy thinking, on the other hand, lacked any major idea or feeling of direction, at least as consciousness would understand it; it went on effortlessly, did not seem to tire the mind, in fact served as a refreshment to an overworked directed thinking; it worked with reminiscences, images rather than speech, feelings rather than concepts; it turned away from external reality, oriented itself toward the past with its memory pictures or toward the future rather than toward the present; it set in motion a subjective stream of fantasy fed by egotistic wishes; it was wholly unproductive as far as adaptation to external, here-and-now reality was concerned. Jung found this type of thinking present in dreams of children and adults, the "lower" races, the people of antiquity, who largely thought mythologically, and in the daydreams of adapted but fatigued, directed-thinking adults of our own day.

Dream or fantasy thinking, in contrast to directed thinking, is never more than partly conscious, as, for example, in daydreams. Fantasy thinking is also present in the unconscious dreams "offered" to consciousness, which psychoanalysis could not clearly interpret. Finally, fantasy thinking is present in the wholly unconscious fantasy systems which dissociated personalities tend to produce.

Previously science had been linked with conscious, directed thinking exclusively oriented toward reality, the publicly available world where universal validity is not implausibly hoped for; whereas subjectively oriented fantasy thinking, to the degree that it had been at all systematized, expressed itself in dreams, fantasies, visions, hallucinations, and superstitions.

In making what amounted to an apology for
psychoanalysis in general and for his own program of
research in particular, Jung now in effect showed that
the science of psychology is directed thinking about
fantasy thinking.

This new understanding of psychology allows the
bridging of these two fundamental operations of the
psyche, bringing some measure of integration to the
individual and ultimately to the culture. Addi-
tionally, it allows a retrieval of the past: we can
see, for instance, that "Oedipus is still a living
thing for all,"[17] and therefore we find ourselves
shocked at this legend just as the ancients were.
Such retrieval shows us all that we are no more moral
than the ancients; consequently, a more just
assessment of ourselves, won by attaining "a stable
point of view outside our own culture,"[18] is made
possible, and thereby is our humanity deepened.
Furthermore, the scientific retrieval allows us to
transcend the sentimental or purely aesthetic approach
to ancient symbolism in myth and religion. A
stripping away of the feelings allows for a more
intelligent comprehension, thus making an ethical
response possible, at least indirectly. Science,
therefore, is a powerful tool in the struggle for
moral autonomy. Thus, as Jung sees it, the cultural
value of the science of dynamic psychology (here
psychoanalysis) is enormous.

The Nature and Function of the Psyche
as Revealed by the Science of Psychology

If in the preceding section we have dealt with
Jung's understanding of the activity and assumptions
of the science of psychology, we must here discuss the

content of his psychology. What did he understand the nature and activity of the psyche or soul to be? Let us consider the psyche under three headings: structure, dynamics, and development (and transformation).

Structure

Jung understands the psychic structure largely in topographical terms. If we start from the waking situation of an individual, we find a structure of awareness we can call conscious personality (or "I-ness") operating in one of the two modes discussed in the preceding section: directed thinking or fantasy thinking. Directed thinking is the paradigmatic mode of consciousness, and the ego, the structure of conscious adaptation to external reality, is most itself in performing in a goal-directed manner. The hero-myth, which is the central myth, expresses the drive toward the paradigmatic activity of conscious personality.

Functioning on he edge of consciousness is fantasy thinking, which, for all its taking place in the daylight world of consciousness, is not fully conscious in that the directedness and goal-orientedness of thought is relaxed and logical relationships give way to fantasy (emotional) connections: images take precedence over words. The fantasy thinking present in waking consciousness is on a continuum with the fantasy thinking of the night dreams, the latter being only "farther away" from conscious control. The imagery and affect are, on the whole, proportionately increased. There remains, however, a link with consciousness such that the fantasy can be recalled through a directed but relaxed

attention. There is, analogically speaking, an
intention on the part of the unconscious systems to
manifest themselves to and for the sake of
consciousness. This level of unconsciousness is to
some degree determined by the events in conscious
life. Memory traces from one's own personal past are
found at this level of the psyche. With the
regression of psychic energy to this individual past,
these memory-traces are activated and dreams produced.

At a yet deeper level, i.e., at that level
farthest away from conscious personality, there are
archaic mental traits, which come to light with the
regression of the psychic energy under strong repres-
sions and introversion psychoses. There may reecho
what was once a manifest expression of psychic life.
This deepest level, which is most distant
historically, is that stratum of psychic life which
properly deserves the designation "unconscious."[19]
Here is an early expression of Jung's later and
pervasive attitude that the unconscious psyche is
truly the trans-individual or collective. This most
archaic psyche is expressed in mythic fragments which
are present in one's own dreams, in the myths of whole
cultures, and in the unconscious fantasy systems which
tend toward and express dissociatedness in the souls
of psychotics.

Dynamics

The dynamic "driving strength of our own soul" is
libido.[20] Jung takes the term current in
psychoanalytic circles largely in the sense of sexual
interest and sexual energy and widens it to refer to
psychic energy in general.[21] He has no hesitation in
linking it with Schopenhauer's <u>will</u>,[22] with the

vitality of the life-process.[23]   Thus, it is the
generalized energy manifest in itself in the varied
functions and expression of psychic life rather than a
specific force.[24]   Jung sees libido as the term in
biology (psychology is here included under the science
of bios)[25] comparable to energy in the natural
sciences. Furthermore, he thinks it promises to unify
the biological sciences in a way comparable to Robert
Mayer's unifying postulation of energy in the natural
sciences.[26]   As a generalized concept, i.e., an
abstraction, it is not experienceable. It must be
manifested as a specific energy or force, but the
reality is not the same as the manifestation. Libido
is a theoretical construct to account for the various
strivings in the human psyche. Jung contrasts at
length his notion of libido as genetic with Freud's
understanding which he characterizes as descriptive.
He means that in contrast to a notion of libido which
is comprised of a plurality of sexual components,[27]
which is too much like the hoary philosophical notion
of a psyche with faculties, one must postulate a
relatively unified psychic energy capable of manifold
applications. Jung does not wish to deny the large
role that sexuality plays as a manifestation of
libido, since libido as passionate desire clearly
manifests itself as sexual desire and need; however,
libido is capable of investing the nutritive function
with energy prior to its activating sexual interest
and development. Furthermore, to give libido an
exclusively sexual coloring is to forfeit any real
possibility of explaining the psychoses in which there
is a loss of interest in external reality in general
and thus of the sexual in particular. Since the
crucial thing in the libido theory, as Jung sees it,

is not the sexual but the energic accent, and since there is a psychic development from one function to others, it is better to replace the descriptive notion of libido (which notion, admittedly, has a certain phenomenological value, i.e., things "appear" this way) with a genetic one (which allows a grouping of the psychic energy as unitary, mobile, and goal-oriented).

With this interpretation it is admitted that libido is capable of self-transformation as it moves from one temporary localization to another. In the normal individual libido develops without serious immobilizing conflict from a pre-sexual stage, characterized almost wholly by the functions of nutrition and growth, as in the first four or five years of life, to a pre-pubertal stage, characterized by the germination of sexuality, to a stage of maturity from puberty on. Along with this there is the successful adaptation of the individual to the tasks of life (not exclusively erotic), characterized by the constant moving of the libido outward and forward. The outward movement of libido is known as extraversion; the reverse is an inward turning or introversion. The forward movement is progression; its reverse, regression. Thus with a dynamic life-energy capable of moving outward and inward, forward and backward, Jung felt he had a key to understanding neurosis (regression of libido from the actual task and a concomitant reactivation of infantile fantasies, often sexual in nature), psychosis (the almost total withdrawal of all interest from the outside world), mythology, religion, and cultural change.

Implicit in the discussion above about the double movement of psychic energy is the notion of the ambivalence of libido, a dynamism opposed to itself, striving forwards and backwards simultaneously, willing destruction as well as life.[28] The libido is the power for beautifying everything and the power for destroying everything.[29] In mythological terms, libido is both God and Devil.[30] This accounts for the contradictory nature of mythologies (heroes beset by hostile brothers, e.g.), moral conflict (good and evil), and psychological illness (extraversion versus introversion).

Libido itself is not observable; however, it comes to expression in the characteristic form of fantasy-- daydreams, night dreams, visions, and hallucinations.[31] In fact, the primary concrete or phenomenal object for scientific investigation is fantasy-imagery and its movement. Jung had been fascinated by fantasy-imagery from his doctoral dissertation (1902) on. However, in his Psychology of the Unconscious it flared into prominence; in fact this work was written while he was awash in the mythology and religion of world cultures. He took it as his task to investigate world mythology as if he were analyzing the fantasies of the insane. Whether or not this is a valid assumption, and whether or not Jung managed to keep his enthusiasm within proper methodological limits--a moot point in both cases-- Jung boldly forayed into a field of fantasy not generally explored by the medical world. If, as previously stated, for Jung the true object of psychology is the unconscious, and the unconscious largely and eminently comes to expression in fantasy, then the investigation of dreams, visions, hallucinations is the proper focus of psychological research.

Jung's notion of the libido as the life-energy
experienced subjectively as desire and intention
through the imagery presented to consciousness serves
as the single and simple schema for interpreting the
mythology of West and East, primitive and civilized:
all symbols may be reduced to "libido and its fixed
primitive qualities."[32] All mythology is capable of
translation into psychology--libido and its endless
transformations, from which it ultimately sprang.[33]
Fantasy, therefore, whether it be of individual
provenance, as in a dream, or of the life of a people
as a whole, as in myth, is the inerrable clue to the
dynamics of psyche.

Development and Transformation

In addition to the structure and dynamics of the
psyche, we must explore Jung's notion of the
development and transformation of psychic energy.
Jung wholeheartedly accepts the evolutionary viewpoint
and applies the biological dictum that "ontogeny
recapitulates phylogeny" to psychology in two ways:
(a) the human psyche has traces of the animal psyche
in it and traverses its animal past in its own development, and (b) the human psyche relives its own
history in the development of each mind.
Psychological experience, growth, and transformation,
whether of individuals or of groups, is part of
biological evolution. Jung sees culture, including
Christianity, as performing a role in the evolution of
the species.[34]

The terminus a quo of the human psyche is "the
animal psyche"; the terminus ad quem is the morally
autonomous or individualized person.[35] Human life is
lived between the termini. At one extreme is the

animal psyche with its reactions and expressions of a
"generally diffused uniformity and solidity,"[36] only
observable in human beings as traces. With respect to
the animal psyche human beings seem enormously
individualized.[37] In the development of the
individual human being, the traits of the animal
psyche are most apparent in the very young (or perhaps
in the mentally ill or senile). That this should be
so is due to the relatively unconscious state of the
child, and, lacking consciousness of any stabilized
sort, the child is not capable of differentiated and
ultimately highly individualized responses.

At the other extreme is the morally autonomous
individual, who acts not out of some compulsion,
religious or otherwise (e.g., for the love of Christ),
but willingly out of knowledge of what necessity
requires. This is perfect freedom.[38] Obviously, only
a few attain this state of heroic individualism since
most accept the delusions of their mythologies and
religious symbols. Jung feels that psychoanalysis is
the way par excellence of transformation toward moral
autonomy. From the perspective of such an individual
the mass of mankind are highly undifferentiated, hence
capable of only standardized, group-approved
responses. In short, they are largely unconscious.
Their motivations stem from, their affections are
directed toward, and their limited transformations are
legitimized by mythologies and religious symbols.

The guiding principle behind his understanding of
psychic development is the evolutionary advance from
the undifferentiated, instinctual response of animals
at the lowest level, of primitive peoples and children
(the primitive has an infantile psychology, according
to Jung) at a higher level, of mature adults contained

within traditional cultural symbols, to the highly
differentiated, morally autonomous individuals, who
possessing "a certain intellectual supremacy" "succeed
in throwing off mythology."[39]

In a previous paragraph we considered the three
stages of development: presexual, prepubertal, and
mature. Further, Jung seems to have some notion of
cultural development that runs contrapuntally to the
earlier two stages and then develops significantly
within the third stage. This is understandable owing
to the relatively long life remaining to the human
organism after sexual maturity. The concern here is
not to work out a highly differentiated "stages of
life" psychology but to raise the question: how does
the libido move from stage to stage? He answers in
effect: by means of the symbol. The symbol is the
great transformer of libido. In general, libido,
which in the early life of individuals and cultures is
invested in a narrow range of objects--parental
figures, meteorological phenomena, etc.--develops or
transforms itself through the product of fantasy analogies. The human mind seemingly has an impulse to
discovery of the environment through analogy.[40] The
fantasy analogy is the symbol. The life-impulse
necessarily creates (posits) new energy-focalizations,
expressed outwardly as tasks, cultural demands, etc.
and inwardly as fantasy images. On the whole, the
outward-turning libido toward objects is normal and
desirable; the inward-turning, pathological. In
neurosis, the individual turns away from a life task
and the libido regresses and activates infantile
reminiscences and symbols are created. In normal
development, the unconscious libido produces fantasy
images in order to prepare the individual for future

life tasks. What distinguishes between the two possibilities is whether the libido lingers on a reactivated image or whether it retreats to the "Realm of the Mothers" in order to move outward into life, refreshed.

The symbolic expressions of religious mythology are so many expressions of the libido and its fate. Christ, Dionysus, Mithras, etc., are all expressions of the individual's libido movement and transformation. Religious symbols have their value in moving one from a fixation on parental imagos to moral autonomy by means of a group mythic identification. Looked at from the perspective of Jung's psychology, the fascination with mythological and religious imagery and ideation, whether outwardly in the approved mythos of the culture or inwardly in the archaic traces drawn from the deepest levels of the psyche, is simply functional to the development of the fully free and independent personality. This theme will be later picked up and amplified, though with some modification, as the individuation process.

The Understanding of Religious Experience in Psychology of the Unconscious

When we turn to our expressed concern, the understanding of religious experience, we find that Psychology of the Unconscious has almost nothing explicit to say; consequently, we must draw out implications from the preceding sections for Jung's understanding. However, one passage directly speaks of the religious experience of persons belonging to ancient cults as "the union with the God of antiquity."[41] First of all, two features of this passage must be noted. An explanatory footnote to

this passage says of "union" that it is "[t]he mystic
feelings of the nearness of God; the so-called
personal inner experience."[42] Religious experience,
therefore, is a matter of the inner feeling of an
individual, of desire (eros) directed to a non-
visible, non-public object, an image. It is not an
intellectual, directed-thinking activity; it provides
no knowledge. The religious experience can provide no
literal information about how things are but can
express psychological truth; it can analogically give
insight into the processes of libido transformation
going on in an individual and with the aid of
psychoanalysis can foster psychological maturation.
The first feature, then, is the non-cognitive, self-
reflexive nature of religious experience. Secondly,
such unio mystica was understood by the ancient cults
as more or less concrete sexual intercourse.[43] In the
ancient, i.e., pre-Christian, world, so Jung avers,
sexuality was an open matter and the religions of the
day were unabashedly erotic. This attitude was
reversed by Christianity, which, "with its repression
of the manifest sexual, is the negative of the ancient
sexual cult."[44] Assuming the uniformitarian position
that the religious dynamic does not significantly
change from culture to culture,[45] Jung in effect
argues that religious experience is nothing but libido
manifested as sexual, repressed as neurotic, or
sublimated as spiritual. It is not that Jung is
encouraging a return to a pagan morality or religion--
he does not think such is viable for civilized human
beings[46]--but that modern people should understand
what religious experience truly is. We experience our
own libido, indirectly, of course, in the movement of
fantasy images, either sexualized or desexualized, in

the religious heroes and their exploits.   In fact, we
never experience anything in religious experience
other than libido in its varied expression.

The primary libido expression in religious
experience is the symbol.   At this point Jung has not
made the distinction he will later make between the
semiotic (sign) and the symbolic (symbol).[47]   For the
present he understands the symbol as a fantasy image
which expresses in analogical fashion the subjective
longing of the libido in terms of desired objects of
the past--parents, heroic individuals, animals,
meteorological phenomena, and other objects of the
environment which have received one's libidinal
interest.   Yet the same image or symbol can be
employed in a two-fold way.   If, on the one hand, the
symbol is a reactivation of memory-traces of, let us
say, one's parent(s) in the regressive flight from
life tasks, and the fixation on the image has the
effect of keeping one stuck, one is and becomes
neurotic and one's religious experience--the intense
feelings projected onto the image which has emerged--
is inevitably neurotic. If, on the other hand, the
symbol is a reactivation of a memory trace, perhaps of
one's parents but more likely of some ancestor or
cultural hero of the past, let us say, Buddha,
Dionysus, Christ, Mithras, in order to move forward
more smoothly into life tasks, then such reactivation
is a sublimation of libido and a building of culture.
Thus, the great religions with their myths, institu-
tional structures, and devotional patterns have played
an enormous biocultural role.

Jung seems to think that religion is a cultural
fact of the past and for all those in the present who
are not capable of freeing themselves from the past

(which means all but a very few of the most
progressive, i.e., scientific, minds of the present).
Religion has had a powerful value-creating and value-
conserving role in culture and should therefore be
appropriately appreciated. Jung seems to be up
against a paradox in that the sublimation necessary
for religion to work successfully employs fictions,
and to employ fictions is to alienate oneself from
one's instincts and thus to disturb adaptation. But
for Jung life is the touchstone for truth, not the
reverse; paradox cannot be rejected out of hand.
Furthermore, Jung thinks that for some unknown reason
the traditional sublimations are no longer working, at
least for many people. For individuals so affected
the appeal of authoritarian religion to belief has to
be replaced by understanding; the symbolism must be
seen for what it is.

The concept of religious experience, consequently,
is an illusion if taken as other than a psychological
projection into a postulated metaphysical space. If
individuals or groups of people are not able to
experience their own libido as their own and to adopt
a moral stance, i.e., take a responsible position,
toward it, then religious experience, whether directly
in inner awareness or indirectly through the cultus,
may provide a socially useful means of transforming
the libido. If the libido, when regressing in order
to escape fulfilling life tasks, collides with the
incest prohibition, then the incest wish, which, as
Jung interprets it, is the desire for the pleasures of
unconsciousness, is sublimated or spiritualized as
love for God. The God-concept is nothing but a
representation of a quantity of libido.[48] In loving
God, in feeling the mystical nearness, we are loving

our own unconscious inheritance which we share with
all human beings.[49]

In Psychology of the Unconscious Jung is
ambivalent: is religious experience to be understood
functionally (as a means of individual psychological
adaptation and development) or genetically (as an
expression of some mysterious pool of ancestral
memory-traces)? Is the viewpoint ontogenetic or
phylogenetic?[50] Two models of the psyche seem to be
struggling for Jung's acceptance. On the one hand, he
accepts from Freud the wish-fulfillment theory and
reiterates the idea expressed in his earlier essay
that "the religious instinct feeds upon the incestuous
libido of the infantile period."[51] Religion is the
systematization of the reactivated infantile libido,[52]
which system is expressed in a manner acceptable to an
ego repressing its sexuality. What is denied one in
reality can be fulfilled in fantasy. On the other
hand, he is hinting toward a later development,
specifically his notion of the collective unconscious,
when he says that religious projections emerge from a
common pool of "archaic inclinations" shared by all
human beings everywhere.[53] The tension between these
viewpoints would require a larger theory for its
resolution.

Religious experience, including its expression in
myths and institutions, is in principle capable of
both positive and negative valuation. Obviously, as a
psychotherapist Jung would tend to see neurosis and
neurotic religion as something which in every case is
to be abominated and to be healed if possible.
Religious experience in this mode would have to be
unmasked for what it is, a cheat.[54] As a sublimation
of erotic interest and as an encouragement to

brotherly compassion,[55] religious experience is culture-enhancing both for the individual and the group and is to be accepted as a positive expressions for the masses of people, i.e., for those not morally capable of a heroic struggle for individualization.[56] It is clear that Jung sees for himself and others of the spiritual and intellectual elite the moral task of understanding rather than believing, of seeing through the myths rather than living in them--and this by means of psychoanalysis. He understands himself as morally beyond traditional Christianity, but in speaking of the aesthetic value of the symbol he reveals unwittingly a nostalgia for it.

Jung's first treatment of religious experience is, therefore, as a species of experience of libido and its transformation. But since there are other possible experiences of libido (aesthetic, for example), what is it that makes religious experience religious? Jung's Psychology of the Unconscious provides no direct or satisfactory answer to this question. Presumably, to the degree that an experience engenders and is expressed by an image of God culturally approved, to that degree it can be called religious. This would be a petitio principii of the rankest sort were it not that Jung intimates that a God-image is a representation of a sum of libido which in some way stands for libido as a whole. Thus, the general attributes of divinity, as he sees it, are omnipotence, a stern, fear-evoking paternalism, and love (either paternalistic, as in Judaism and Christianity, or maternalistic, as in religions devoted to the Mother Goddess). In some cases theriomorphic traits express mysterious aspects of deity. The idea of God, which Jung claims is

> [A] thought which humanity in every part of
> the world and in all ages has brought forth
> from itself and always again anew in similar
> forms; a power in the other world to which
> man gives praise, a power which creates as
> well as destroys . . .[57]

is a thought which is "necessary to life."[58] The
reason for its importance and pervasiveness, it would
seem, is that the God-idea has hitherto been the most
comprehensive expression of the libido; and,
presumably, the reason why a God-image is necessary is
that there is an evolutionary drive toward the
realizing of the telos of an organism which on the
human level occurs only in and through the
transformation of consciousness.

Jung will never again emphasize dynamics over form
as much as he does in Psychology of the Unconscious.
He admits here to complexes, which are quite
consistent over time;[59] he will speak of the "fixed
primitive qualities" of libido;[60] but it is clear that
preeminence is given to the dynamism of libido and its
capacity for contradictory self-expression. Such
symbolic chaos does not concern Jung as it would if he
were trying to correlate fantasy-images to each other.
Rather all symbols are ultimately interchangeable
expressions of the one transcending, dynamic libido.
By 1919 Jung had begun to speak of "archetypes,"[61] and
more and more the structure of the unconscious became
a theme for him. The laval flow of ideas finds a more
manageable channel, and the libido is increasingly
seen as structured as well as structurable. The flow
is never denied, but more and more it is seen as
patterned.

The Theory Reconsidered and Rounded Out [62]

In 1928 Jung published a lengthy essay entitled "On Psychic Energy," which had been planned shortly after he had published the Psychology of the Unconscious in 1912. Owing to the greater importance of working out the type problem (if Psychology of the Unconscious had cost Jung his relationship with Freud, then Psychological Types became necessary for understanding inter alia why the relationship failed), Jung laid aside the "The Theory of the Libido" (the original title) until some time in 1927. The work was deemed necessary owing to the misunderstandings and even outright rejection which the original treatment had produced. [63] Jung took pains to establish the legitimacy of the energic viewpoint, accepted in natural science, in psychology; he showed the applicability of this viewpoint to the data of psychological investigation; he worked out the various movements and transformations of libido; and, finally, he related the concept as he employed it to primitive conceptions, hence rooting it in early attempts of the human mind to understand its world. [64]

Metascientific Reflection

First of all, Jung is engaged in metascientific reflection. (On occasion Jung will, surprisingly, granted his anti-metaphysical bias, speak of the "metaphysical aspect" of notion of libido. [65] The import, however, is more generalized-theoretical than ontological.) Characteristically, Jung does not write a treatise on metapsychology but provides only the reflection needed to make his position understandable; thus, no comprehensive account is given. His reflections center around three themes: viewpoint, model, and the nature of scientific language.

Scientific Viewpoint

The psychologist wishes to know what is unknown nature, viz., the psyche. There is no independent means for "getting at it"; one must use psyche to explor psyche. But the psyche of the observer is limited and, to some degree, subjectively biased; the observer has a viewpoint (<u>Anschauung</u>), a perspective on the psyche. The perspective is determined by three things: (1) the observable world, (2) the a priori conditions of thinking in general (here he assumes the general validity of Kant's critical philosophy), and (3) the psychological attitude of the observer.

The first determinant is the givenness of the observable world, which for the psychologist is the psyche. If the psyche were simply subjective--and no one doubts that the psyche has to do with human subjectivity however defined--it would be incapable of investigation; however, the psyche is in some important sense objective and objectifiable. This means that there are psychic processes and events which observers can investigate and that theories can be constructed and applied to psychic phenomena intersubjectively given. Some theories can be shown to be inadequate in light of such data. Responsible scientific work requires that a theory attempt to explain the facts as currently known. It is important to emphasize this aspect in that throughout his career Jung was charged with engaging in speculation loosed from its moorings in empirical reality.

A second determinant is the a priori conditions of human thought. Jung claimed that Kant's critical philosophy was "the mother of modern (read 'analytical') psychology."[66] This statement admits of a double interpretation. On the one hand, this is a historical judgment about Jung's own intellectual development; and, on the other, it expresses a metascientific conviction about the nature of scientific activity: things in themselves cannot be investigated and thus known; whatever is known and knowable is cognized and cognizable through the limitations of the human mind. Knowledge is necessarily species-specific. As a student, Jung had read Kant assiduously, and such a viewpoint allowed him to criticize the dogmatism of both theology (in which he was raised) and scientific materialism (in which he was trained). Jung later referred to himself as a Kantian and tended to identify epistemological criticism—a necessity of responsible science—with Kant. While some interpreters have doubted the radicality of Kant's alleged effect on Jung or Jung's intellectual dependence on Kant,[67] the truth seems to be that the transcendental perspective was so fundamental for Jung that even when he was not alluding to Kant by name or making direct references to the Critiques he was indirectly trading on Kant's capital and was able to generate transcendental insights and criticisms of his own.[68] Admittedly, Jung was not simply a Kantian and recognized Kant's limitations.[69] Nevertheless, Kant's doctrine of epistemological limitation remained fundamental to Jung's work as a scientist and metascientist.[70]

The third determinant of scientific viewpoint—and here Jung among the psychologists of his time was most insightful—was the psychological attitude of the observer. In fact Jung claimed that the relative dominance of a viewpoint depends more on the psychological attitude, the characteristic "set" of the individual scientist than upon the objective behavior of the phenomena.[71] Jung had been led or driven to such a view out of his intellectual struggle with Freud, with the conflict between Adler and Freud, which he had observed and, more personally, had participated in. With the break with Freud the working out of a typology, which would allow for divergences of temperament and characteristic functioning, became an existential necessity. While it had been anciently known that thinkers as persons were individually different, Jung argued that therefore thinkers as thinkers were incommensurably different. Not only reason and experience but also the psychological set of the thinker determined scientific theory and all other intellectual activity as well.[72] In fact, theories are articulated expressions of viewpoints. One of Jung's complaints against philosophers is that they are incognizant of who does the thinking so mesmerized are they by the norms of universality and rationality.[73] Whether or not Jung has fully seen not only the force of his insight but also its limitation is a matter for further consideration. Jung tends to leave the philosopher and other intellectual workers little ground on which to argue the matter. Whether he allowed for levels of universality in rationality is somewhat debatable since he was convinced of the unconscious, hence uncontrollable and paradoxical, roots of rationality.[74]

Model

Jung's non-positivist[75] reading of what a
scientist does allows him to look at theorizing as
model building. Even though he more
characteristically at this stage spoke of "viewpoint"
rather than model, his intention is roughly the same
as that of Ian Barbour, a contemporary scientist-
theologian, who defines a model as "a symbolic
representation of selected aspects of the behavior of
a complex system for particular purposes." No literal
description of the world is intended; rather, a model
is "an imaginative tool for ordering experience." A
model is partly based on analogy with the familiar and
partly is the creation of something new, for which no
rules can be given.[76] As early as 1913 Jung had
spoken of his concept of libido as a model, and he
continued throughout his career to consider himself as
making models.[77] Later Jung tended to contrast
asserting (saying that X is so) and constructing
models (saying that if you look at the world this way
you will see such-and-such).[78] Jung clearly believes
that models are heuristically valuable in observation,
but he is not consistently clear whether the models
make ontological claims even lightly proposed. In
certain ways Jung's position sounds instrumentalistic;
that is, theories are understood not as making any
claim about what is the case but only as possessing
utilitarian value for unearthing data, correlating
observations, or suggesting certain predictions.[79]
Models on this approach are understood as useful fictions, creative products of the mind indeed but
lacking explanatory power. However, it is clear that
for Jung the viewpoint or model in some sense

coincides with the _explicanda_, else the theory articulating such would be inapplicable in practice.[80] Jung is convinced that there is some correlation between responsible theories and facts. Jung's practice reveals that his real view is more a critical realism in which the model and the derived theory re-present the world, in which theories can be true as well as useful, in which science explores and discovers as well as constructs and invents, and in which one seeks to understand as well as (when applicable) to predict or to control.[81] Models and the resulting theories are necessarily selective, incomplete, and abstract. They are symbolic constructs devised for specific purposes. They are creative products of the human mind; nevertheless, when responsibly entertained and elaborated, these models can and do correspond to the world because the world has the structure that it does.[82] His employment of a particular model of the psyche will be worked out in a later passage.

The Nature of Scientific Concepts

A third issue in the meta-science of the essay is the nature of scientific concepts. There is a necessary concretization of abstract concepts in science whenever these are applied. Then it appears that a substance is posited. For example, if one speaks of a quantum of energy, the imagination, which can never be expunged from scientific thinking, represents it as a quantum of something. This is apparently unavoidable.[83] Both physics and psychology deal with the concept of energy, which has two roots. On the one hand, as pure, the concept of energy, like time, is an immediate, a priori, intuitive idea; the mind supplies the category. On the other hand, as applied, energy is a concrete, empirical concept abstracted from experience, which is the case with all scientific concepts.[84] As pure, the concept has to be understood abstractly as the relations of movement; it is quantitative. Intensities can be measured precisely in the natural sciences through mathematics or estimated in psychology through comparison of relative intensities. Energy in this sense is inexperienceable.

As an applied concept psychic energy is understood qualitatively, by which Jung means that it is experienced as a particular kind of energy--as sexual energy, mental energy, the drive for power and success, and so on. Jung is concerned that the specific energies, the qualitative graspings of the quantitative unknown, be allowed their several identities. The energies of the psyche are plural; psychic energy is one.

The metascientific implication is that if science is to be, as it should, truly explanatory and also to provide for the conceptual freedom necessary for theorizing, then no concrete energy can be identified with the abstract concept (Freud's mistake, so Jung thought). As in the parallel case of physics, the abstract concept of psychic energy allows all psychologists to develop theories, or at least hypotheses, based on the models which their own observations and imaginative thinking suggest.

The Energic Viewpoint

Jung's metascientific reflections were put forth only to justify his own theoretical position: the energic viewpoint, or, alternatively, libido.[85] Jung is convinced that the psyche is too complex and too extensive to be grasped by a single theory. The activity of the psyche is ambiguous, if not paradoxical: "One and the same process takes on different aspects according to the different standpoints from which it is viewed."[86] Jung notes two major standpoints in the natural sciences: the mechanical-causal and the energic-final. The difference depends on what principle of explanation is appealed to, whether it be efficient causality or finality (goal-orientedness). Both principles are necessary in the sciences; and while the "theoretically inadmissible compromise" of considering a process both in terms of cause-effect and means-end produces all kinds of theoretical hybrids, it does give a more or less accurate picture of reality.[87] Jung further notes that both points of view are operative in psychology with Freud's mechanism and Adler's finalism.

Like Adler, Jung takes teleology as his explanatory principle. It is not that there are no causal determinants; there are. But for the specific purpose in mind, viz., the explanation of a vital process, the teleological point of view is to be preferred, and preference between competing viewpoints can be determined only by expediency, i.e., the possibility of obtaining results.[88]

Jung's energic viewpoint or theory of libido is developed from the model of the psyche imaged as "a continuous flow or current of life."[89] It is like a stream of energy. Jung acknowledges a semantic similarity (at least) between his notion of libido and Schopenhauer's will, Aristotle's hormē, Plato's eros, and Bergson's élan vital.[90] He can speak of the

forward movement of this energy in analogy with a
mountain watercourse flowing into a valley. [91] Such a
model sanctions a theory which views the psyche
energically and finalistically, as discussed above,
because in part Jung considered the future as more
important than the past in understanding human
personality development and transformation.
Furthermore, in therapeutic psychology the evidence
for the theory is the transformation of personality
from fragmentariness to ever-increasing wholeness.
Jung would not allow a bifurcation of the science of
personality (in which the theory could be true but its
application effects no healing) and the transformation
of personality (in which persons might be healed but
no claims for the truth of the theory can be made).
Theory and practice are thus understood as external
checks for each other.

At a somewhat more theoretical level Jung borrows
the notion of energy used in the natural sciences,
particularly physics. Here energy is seen as a
dynamism in a relatively closed system. Notions of
actual and potential, forces and states, equivalence
and transformation are suggested. Combining these
disparate perceptions Jung arrives at a theoretical
model of the psyche as a teleologically ordered,
relatively closed energy system.

Jung's theory of libido is rooted in the model so
described in that the meaning of the theoretical terms
is derived from the model, not from observation. [92] At
times, in the fashion of good positivists and naive
realists, Jung suggested that he abstracted his
theoretical terms from observational data. He did not
really do so, but as a de facto critical realist, if
not an instrumentalist, he constructed a theory on the

basis of a model considered relevant to the data. His
scientific theory considers the psyche to be a
teleologically ordered, relatively closed energy
system. Concepts such as energy, teleology, an energy
system only relatively closed, and transformation of
energy are all derived from the model of a flow of
vital energy, not directly from any data. Arguing by
analogy, Jung infers that operative are the principles
of conservation of energy ("the sum total of energy
remains constant and is susceptible neither of
increase nor of decrease") and the principle of
equivalence ("for a given quantity of energy expended
or consumed in bringing about a certain condition, an
equal quantity of the same or another form of energy
will appear elsewhere").[93] The principle of
equivalence is particularly important heuristically in
actual psychological treatment as when, for example, a
transference suddenly disappears, but the patient is
then all of a sudden plagued by an equally disturbing
outbreak of new and stubborn symptoms. Furthermore,
the intensity of energy movement in one direction
(progression, for example) reappears in the intensity
of the reversed movement of energy (regression).
Other principles and assumptions are the difference in
potential between two systems of energy, the
polaristic nature of energy systems (opposition is
necessary for energy flow), entropy ("transformations
of energy lead to an equalization of differences"),[94]
the quantification of value (differences in values are
differences in intensities of energy since "values are
quantitative estimates of energy"),[95] and the
compensatory relation between conscious and
unconscious systems.

Structural Aspects of Life

The above-mentioned principles are expressions of
the behavior of the flow of energy; the accent falls
on the dynamic movement in the psyche. In his
Psychology of the Unconscious (1912) Jung emphasized
dynamics over form to such a degree that everything
seemed to collapse into everything else: all symbols
are ultimately reducible to the flow of libido.
Thereafter, and for a complex of reasons, Jung
increasingly gave attention to form, to patterns of
psychic energy; structural elements seemed to
dominate. Four of such elements will be delineated
below.

First of all, the experiencing subject is re-
identified as a partial energy system exhibiting goal-
directed behavior. That is, in re-identification the
context of presuppositions shifts, which according to
some philosophers of science is the necessary
indication of a theoretical explanation (an
explanation is not just a translation of one set of
terms into another within the same context of
presuppositions).[96] We must therefore consider the
experiencer not as a subject with an immediate sense
of selfhood, moral agency, ontological awareness,
etc., but as if he/she were an energy system
interacting with other systems with resulting
redistributions of energy.

The images and series of images--especially those
which stand out in the stream of experiencing because
of their striking visual or auditory qualities and
their peculiar juxtaposition of contrary features both
of which elicit high interest in the subject--are
theoretically re-identified as symbols, primordial
images, or archetypal images. Accordingly, the symbol

is the second structural element. Contrary to what our ego or waking consciousness assumes, symbols appearing on the fringe of consciousness, phenomenologically speaking, have substance; they have a certain thickness and endure over time. The subject can interact with them and in so doing be transformed.

The third structural element is the archetype. Archetypes are the dominants or constants in the total energy system; they are enduring patterns of energy, which have in addition to the specific energy needed to maintain themselves a "supplementary charge"[97] or quantum of disposable energy, which makes possible the effecting of the archetypal imagery. It is important to note that the archetypes are unexperienced and unexperienceable constructs. Like electrons, they are postulated as existing, not posited. For Jung the archetypes are postulates of the psychic system theoretically necessary to account for the identity and the universality of symbols. Whether the archetypes exist extra-linguistically, i.e., beyond the formal requirements of a theoretical system as features of the "real" world, can be asserted only as a probability. Whether there is anything like a one-to-one correlation between the postulated archetype of theory and reality cannot be known.

The fourth structural element is the disposable energy or libido flowing in the whole system. Energy appears in various configurations and in various degrees of fluidity. It is capable of movement in different directions with varying intensities and velocities. The psyche is inherently dissociable; thus there may be multiple energies moving in different directions simultaneously.

Explanation of Religious Experience

On the basis of the foregoing, how is religious experience to be explained? The experience of some God-image or other mythological symbol is the experience of a paradoxical and powerful quantum of libido. It is paradoxical in that the ancient past is the imaginative indication of the future development of the personality. The symbol functions as a God-image, the norm for all religious experiences, when this particular quantum is taken to represent the whole system. The part functions for the whole if and only if it (a) expresses all the possible movements of psychic energy (as in a symbol which paradoxically combines past and future, good and evil, male and female, wrath and grace, etc.), (b) evokes the greatest possible interest in the experiencer, and (c) effects the transformation of the energy from one state to another. Therefore, religious experience in general and the experience of God in particular are never _of_ anything more or other than libido and its endless transformation.

Though Jung will develop (only partially, it must be admitted) two other models of the psyche and the theories based on them, Jung never abandoned the notion of the psyche as an energy system,[98] nor the notion of the archetype as a non-observable entity postulated to account for observable effects,[99] nor the understanding of the science as the "phenomenology of psychic dominants."[100] In his later years Jung was greatly encouraged to find that many of the presuppositions of modern physics squared with his understanding of the unconscious psyche. Furthermore, Jung continued to think of the experience of God as the experience of one content among others in the collective unconscious.[101] At times he identified the experience of God as the experience of the collective unconscious as a totality.[102] Within this model and the theory issuing from it the experience of God is the experience of a natural content/process, albeit of a special and important sort. For all theoretical and practical purposes, God is that aspect of the psyche which is unmanageable, beyond rational control. Whether the "God" has any ontological status beyond the psyche cannot be known by science, nor could this knowledge, if it existed, make any difference to the individual. For the purpose of human life, it is knowledge enough that something in the collective unconscious having some affinities with the traditional theological object should and does encounter and transform individuals.

As will be shown in succeeding chapters, Jung operated with at least two other theories of religious experience. The reasons for doing so will be more properly spelled out there. However, granted his concerns of therapy, the numinous as he later came to understand it, and the integrity and fate of individuals and even Western culture, Jung inevitably and, I will argue, necessarily pushed beyond the confines of the scientific-psychological theory. For the present it is enough to point out some internal reasons for finding as less than adequate the scientific-psychological theory based on the model of the stream or continuous flow of vital energy. In reidentifying the human subject as an energy system, even though a vital one, the person has been lost. The specific qualitative aspects of personhood such as self-conscious knowing, valuing, intending, and deciding have been reduced to sub-(pre-)personal processes. At best, the life surge, the elan vital, is accounted for, but the specifics of choice and decision are inadequately addressed and comprehended. One might attempt to relate the two models of vital energy and personal decision as genus and species, as ground (presupposition) and consequent; or one might distinguish as in process philosophy between the transition aspect and the concrescence aspect, the macroscopic species and microscopic species of process;[103] or, again, one might find some other novel and fruitful way of bringing into contiguity but maintaining the important distinction between these two models. At any rate, as it stands the stream of vital energy model does not properly distinguish and specify the distinctive features of personal experiencing.

Not only is the stream model sub-(or pre-) personal, it is implicitly and inconsistently non-personal in that for the scientific-psychological theory to work all traces of selfhood would have to be expunged or at least cancelled out, which Jung could not do. Tacitly presupposed is the unique selfhood of the scientific observer, of the members of the scientific community, and of the interested lay public. It is a self, not simply a vital energy system, which is observing, making models, interpreting other selves as systems of psychic energy, evaluating data, models, and theories, and the like. Selfhood or personality is a more primitive notion than the stream model or the theory of the psyche as a relatively closed, teleologically ordered system of vital energy. The more basic cannot be a specification of the less basic. One alternative to this less than satisfactory outcome would be to interpret process, at least at the human level, in terms of the decisions of subjects, something like the Whiteheadian tradition has done.

Finally, the attempt to treat quality in terms of quantity is highly problematic. Consider, for example, Jung's quantitative definition of will. "I regard the will as the amount of psychic energy (psychische Energiesumme) at the disposal of consciousness" (emphasis added).[104] Furthermore, value as psychic intensity is a quantitative notion ("Values are quantitative estimates of energy").[105] Values are in effect reducible to facts, and Jung is stuck with a species of the naturalistic fallacy. We need not explore this objection further here. Jung's saving grace is that he makes qualitative assumptions--his anthropology is richer than his science--that undergird his more quantitative and abstracted scientific-psychological observations and theories; and because of this Jung must provide a more fundamental theory or theories, which the next two chapters will present. But for the moment it has to be said that Jung's first theory, for whatever heuristic value it may have, severely limps in its reduction of selfhood to sub-(or pre-)personal process, of the observed other to an energy system, and of quality to quantity.

1

Jung, CW 18:662.

2

Ibid., CW 663.

3

The inclusion in Jung's Collected Works of only the revision of his germinal Wandlungen und Symbole der Libido (1912) unfortunately obscures his development and makes it more difficult to see that the scientific-psychological theory of religious experience has a strong early rooting in Jung's thought. I have chosen, therefore, to make all references to the 1916 English translation of the German original Psychology of the Unconscious, tr. B. M Hinckle (New York: Dodd, Mead and Company, 1965).

4

Other and later texts might be profitably consulted, viz., "On the Nature of the Psyche" (1947) in CW 8:159-234, in which Jung restates, somewhat systematically, insights expressed elsewhere as well as making certain explicitations about the nature of the archetype. Further, he speaks of the God-image as corresponding "to a definite complex of psychological facts, and is thus a quantity (eine bestimmte Grosse) which we can operate with"(ibid., p. 279). Whether or not the term translated as "quantity" has any systematic or technical significance is difficult to assess. If it does, the point made restates a thesis of the scientific-psychological theory that quality is translatable into quantity. If it does not, and the God-image is simply to be understood as "a definite something," the point is consistent with the scientific-psychological theory in that whatever can be asserted of God psychologically is necessarily an included part of the inclusive psychic whole. Either way, the evidence suggests that Jung is operating with the same model as found in his writings between 1911 and 1928. Equally as strong a case can be made by appeal to the Memories, Dreams, Reflections, the relevant part written in 1959, where Jung explicitly makes use of the energic model of the psyche (p. 350). The scientific-psychological theory as an expression of this model, once made explicit, was never really repudiated.

5

It is known that the years between 1910 and 1913 were fateful for Jung and that his own ideas were changing. One can interpret the 1912 lectures as a further step away from the largely "anti-Freudian" Psychology of the Unconscious toward Jung's own

psychology [I owe this designation to Professor Peter
Homans, whose work on the Jung-Freud conflict is
highly illuminating. See his Jung in Context
(Chicago: University of Chicago Press, 1979), p. 26.].
This is no doubt true, and it is instructive to
contrast the differences. See James W. Heisig,
Imago Dei: A Study of C. G. Jung's Psychology of
Religion, Studies in Jungian thought, ed. James
Hillman (Lewisburg, Penn.: Bucknell University Press,
1979), p. 29. However, for my purpose here the
similarities are striking, and the Fordham Lectures
primarily make explicit the energic model Jung was
using in Psychology of the Unconscious (see ibid.).

6

Consider Jung's comments about the genesis and
significance of this early work: "I have never felt
happy about this book, much less satisfied with it: it
was written at top speed, amid the rush and press of
my medical practice, without regard to time or method.
I had to fling my material hastily together, just as I
found it. There was no opportunity to let my thoughts
mature. The whole thing came upon me like a landslide
that cannot be stopped. The urgency that lay behind
it became clear to me only later: it was the explosion
of all those psychic contents which could find no
room, no breathing space, in the constricting
atmosphere of Freudian psychology and its narrow
outlook. I have no wish to denigrate Freud, or to
detract from the extraordinary merits of his
investigation of the individual psyche. But the
conceptual framework into which he fitted the psychic
phenomenon seemed to me unendurably narrow. I am not
thinking here of his theory of neurosis, which can be
as narrow as it pleases if only it is adequate to the
empirical facts, or of his theory of dreams, about
which different views may be held in all good faith; I
am thinking more of the reductive causalism of his
whole outlook, and the almost complete disregard of
the teleological directedness which is so
characteristic of everything psychic. . . .Thus
this book became a landmark, set up on the spot where
two ways divided." CW 5:xxiii-xxiv.

7

Jung to Victor White, O.P., 5 October 1945,
Letters, 1:383. Cf. also: "Here it is not to be
forgotten we are moving entirely in the territory of
psychology, which in no way is allied to
transcendentalism, either in positive or negative
relation. It is a question here of relentless
fulfillment of the standpoint of the theory of
cognition, established by Kant, not merely for the

theory, but, what is more important, for the
practice..." Psychology of the Unconscious, 1916, p.
529, n. 42. This is quoted by the editors of the
Letters, 1:384, n. 4, as Jung's direction to the
addressee to consult for his "gnoselogical standpoint
at that time" (ibid.).

    8
    See preceding note for an early statement of his
metaphysical neutralism. In addition, Jung's claim to
neutrality regarding transcendental theories (as in
religion) must be accepted with caution. There is a
defensible distinction between psychology and
philosophy. However, Jung's polemic forced him into a
"poisoning of the wells" of the metaphysician by his
own positivism. There is no way, granted his
assumptions about reality, that Jung could allow
metaphysical statements to be literally meaningful or
true. Thus, his neutralism, while understandable as a
rhetorical device, is as a serious claim to truth
empty posturing. Jung later admitted that he "began
[his] career with repudiating everything that smelt of
belief. That explains my critical attitude in my
Psychology of the Unconscious. You should know that
this book was written by a psychiatrist for the
purpose of submitting the necessary material to his
psychiatric colleagues, material which would
demonstrate to them the importance of religious
symbolism. My audience then was a thoroughly
materialistic crowd, and I would have defeated my own
ends if I had set out with a definite creed or with
definite metaphysical assertions. I was not and I did
not want to be anything else but one of them." Jung
to Victor White, O.P., 5 October 1945, Letters, 1:383.
He continues: "My personal view [about the divine
entity] is that man's vital energy or libido is the
divine pneuma all right and it was this conviction
which it was my secret purpose to bring into the
vicinity of my colleagues' understanding." Ibid., p.
384. However, a careful reading of Psychology of the
Unconscious and relevant letters of the period,
especially to Freud, suggests little of secret agency,
at least with respect to his psychiatric colleagues,
but more, rather, of ambition, the commitment of a
believer, and the joie de combat. It is entirely
possible that a highly gifted young man riding what
was to be a "wave of the future" was for a period
neither what he was before nor was later to become. I
am not fully convinced by Jung's retrospective self-
interpretation. I suspect that the powerful genius of
Freud and the circumstances of youth, "the cause,"

professional success, and international acclaim had their effect on Jung's unsolidified self and thought.

9
   Jung, CW 4:141.
10
   Jung, Psychology of the Unconscious, p. 68.
11
   Jung often discusses reductionism in the context of the question of the legitimacy of translating metaphysical into scientific (psychological) statements, the trans-psychic into the intra-psychic. See, e.g., his "A Psychological Approach to the Trinity," CW 11: 109-200, especially p. 180, for his statement on the necessity of psychological reduction. Jung obviously thinks that reduction legitimate because it creates another and independent order of value, viz., knowledge, a value which Jung along with the modern West holds in high esteem. To understand and, to the degree possible, to control the world is not less than, in fact is more than, the passive acceptance of the world, so modern sophisticates argue. Thus, reductionism is seen in principle to be a valuable move. The obvious but baffling question is, how valuable?

12
   Jung, Psychology of the Unconscious, p. 105.
13
   Ibid., p. 120.
14
   Ibid., p. 263.
15
   Ibid., pp. 198, 199.
16
   Ibid., p. 199.
17
   Ibid., p. 5.
18
   Ibid.
19
   Ibid., p. 37.
20
   Ibid., p. 128.
21
   Jung professes reluctance to introduce new terminology on the assumption that it creates confusion in science, hence his preference for pouring new wine into old wineskins, as here with "libido." Of course, he can argue that classically libido meant simply desire or pleasure. Cf. Sallust's usage which Jung wholeheartedly approves: "They took more pleasure [libidem habebant] in handsome arms and war horses

than in harlots and revelry" (Catilina, 7, tr. by J. C. Rolfe, in Works, Loeb Classical Library [London: William Heinemann, 1921], pp. 14-15. This is quoted in CW 4:247.

22
    Jung, Psychology of the Unconscious, pp. 135-136.

23
    Jung, CW 4: 125.

24
    Ibid.

25
    Jung can speak of libido as "biological energy." CW 4:249.

26
    This is Jung's first mention of Robert Mayer's concept of energy, which analogue will enormously stimulate Jung's thinking; the 1929 essay "On Psychology of the Unconscious," p. 138.

27
    Jung, CW 4:112.

28
    Jung, Psychology of the Unconscious, p. 480.

29
    Ibid., p. 116.

30
    Ibid., p. 120.

31
    Jung's primary concern is that modification of the psyche known as fantasy; however, he never overlooked the importance of bodily expression of the psyche, as in the "set" of person's body (facial expression, gesture, movement, etc.) or in psychosomatic illness. CW 4:248.

32
    Jung, Psychology of the Unconscious, p. 105.

33
    Ibid., p. 120.

34
    It is worth noting that Jung's attitude toward the role of Christianity in the psychic economy of the Western world is ambivalent. For the psychologically immature it has great value in that religious projections can effectively serve those who do not see them as projections. For the psychologically mature the "illusions" of and for the masses do not suffice, particularly because the religious insights are wedded with an outmoded morality. Nevertheless there is great beauty and wisdom in the traditional teachings. He writes: "The Christian religion seems to have fulfilled its great biological purpose, in so far as we are able to judge.

It has led human thought to independence, and has lost
its significance, therefore, to a yet undetermined
extent. . . . It seems to me that we might still make
use in some way of its form of thought, and especially
of its great wisdom of life, which for two thousand
years has proven to be particularly efficacious. The
stumbling block is the unhappy combination of religion
and morality. That must be overcome." Psychology of
the Unconscious, p. 85. (emphasis his).

35
     Jung, CW 4:284. Cf. Nietzsche's view: "Man is a
rope, tied between beast and overman (Übermensch)--a
rope over an abyss. . . . What is great in man is
that he is a bridge and not an end. . . .", Thus Spake
Zarathustra, in The Portable Nietzsche, ed. and trans.
Walter Kaufmann (New York: Viking Press, 1954), pp.
126-27. For the impact Nietzsche made on Jung see
Memories, Dreams, Reflections, p. 102.

36
     Jung, Psychology of the Unconscious, p. 198.

37
     Ibid.

38
     Ibid., p. 262.

39
     Ibid., p. 30.

40
     Ibid., p. 156.

41
     Ibid., p. 256.

42
     Ibid., p. 529, n. 35.

43
     Ibid., p. 256.

44
     Ibid., p. 257.

45
     Ibid., p. 256.

46
     Ibid., p. 238.

47
     Later (1921) he will say: "What Freud terms
symbols are no more than signs for elementary
instinctive processes. But a symbol is the best
possible expression for something that cannot be
expressed otherwise than by a more or less close
analogy." CW 6:63, n. 44).

48
     Jung, Psychology of the Unconscious, p. 71.

49
     Ibid., pp. 200-201.

50

I draw on James Heisig's distinctions here between the functional (final cause) and the genetic (material cause) approaches as well as between the ontogenetic and phylogenetic focus. See his Imago Dei, pp. 23, 24.

51

Jung, Psychology of the Unconscious, p. 71. His reference is to "The Significance of the Father in the Destiny of the Individual," CW 4:301-323. Jung refers to a general theme of the 1909 article, not its exact wording. Thou h Jung would later radically revise this article, at the time of the original publication he understood the individual personality as the focus of the scientific investigation of the psyche. It was, he said later, as if the individual was unique and "rooted in nothing." With the discovery of the collective unconscious the individualized complexes of the personality were seen to be embedded in a general human precondition, an inherited biological structure of the organism. A substratum which is instinctually pre-established. "Foreword to the Third Edition" [1948], CW 4:302.

52

Jung, Psychology of the Unconscious, p. 99.

53

Ibid., pp. 28, 35-36.

54

Ibid., p. 261.

55

Ibid., p. 77.

56

Ibid., p. 262.

57

Cf. Peter Homans' comment:"Jung's quest for a 'stable point of view' and for the 'beauty of symbol' are expressions of nostalgia not achievements of interpretation," in Jung in Context, p. 68.

58

Jung, Psychology of the Unconscious, p. 71.

59

Ibid., p. 198.

60

Ibid., p. 105.

61

For historical information about Jung's use of "archetype" see editorial note at CW 8:133.

62

Some justification is perhaps needed for considering the 1928 treatment of the libido theory as the complement of and fulfillment of the 1912

position, especially in light of the fact that Jung
both personally and conceptually had gone through
massive changes. He had become C. G. Jung, no longer
an advocate of psychoanalysis but the founder and
leader of a new movement in psychology (cf. Peter
Homans, Jung in Context, p. 89) and had developed a
whole new understanding of being human, which was
expressed in a set of new ideas ("archetype,"
"extravert," "introvert," "individuation process,"
"shadow," "anima/animus," "self," "collective
unconscious," etc.). By the time of the second essay
Jung had moved from a rationalistic, reductionistic,
anti-theistic bias to a more open approach in the
psychology of religion. He had shifted from viewing
the psyche largely as an individual affair to seeing
it as the collective matrix of experience. But with
regard to the theory of religious experience the
continuities outweigh the discontinuities: (1) he is
operating with the same model and theory; (2) the
status of the psychic dominants (archetypes) remains
roughly the same; and (3) the characteristic way of
understanding religious experience is basically the
same. As I argued earlier, I am not primarily
approaching Jung with a chronological-developmental
viewpoint; rather, the emphasis on relatively
perduring elements and angles of vision as can be
comprehended in models is my preferred approach.

63
    Jung, CW 8:3.
64
    For a further clarification of his intentions in
the 1928 article, see Jung, MDR, pp. 208-209.
65
    Jung, CW 8:30.
66
    Jung, CW 11: 475.
67
    Consider, for example, the interpretation of
James Heisig, a thoroughly informed and sympathetic
yet critical interpreter. He sees Jung as finding
Kant helpful for his own program but as employing him
without a detailed and highly accurate understanding.
The inaccuracies and sometimes sloppiness in Jung's
appeal to Kant suggest that Jung had only a modest
knowledge of or limited investment in Kant.
Furthermore, though both Jung and Kant espouse a
quasi-subjectivism in epistemology [so Heisig],
similarity does not imply deep influence. Jung is not
so much a Kantian as he is enlisting Kant for a
defense of an epistemological position which Jung
finds compatible and authoritative. See his Imago

Dei, pp. 112, 196-198. Even if Heisig's judgment
should stand, this does not mean, however, that Jung
did not think from the critical-philosophical
perspective stemming from Kant. I am inclined to
think that Kant was a very important factor in Jung's
development and thought, but not as a precise and
scholarly source. Jung tended to make creative use of
many of his sources, not critical one. Thus he seems
unconscious of what appears to have been a filtering
of Kant through various Neo-Kantian lenses, seen, for
example, in his panpsychic constructionism, in his
anti-metaphysicalism, in his making of critical
epistemology the foundational cognitive discipline, in
his belief in the direct imperceivability of, hence
agnosticism about, the extra-psychic world (at least
in some moods), and in his notion of the virtual
nonexistence of the humanly unknown world. See, e.g.,
his Memories, Dreams, Reflections, pp. 255-256.
While Jung himself has almost no direct citations of
recognized Neo-Kantians (he has only one reference
each to Natorp, Cohen, and Rickert, and these are of
uncertain import), his close friend and collaborator
Toni Wolff draws heavily on Rickert's methodological
doctrine in her Studien zu C. G. Jungs Psychologie
(Zurich : Rhein-Verlag, 1959), p. 172.

68
   In his perceptive study of Jung's relation to
Kant, David Brent has asked whether or not Jung's
adoption of Kant's transcendental method as the model
for his psychology was a conscious borrowing. He
writes: "as a conscious Kantian in certain respects,
Jung was more of a Kantian than he himself recognized.
His reading of Kant struck him to the very core, so
much that he could produce out of himself Kantian type
insights without necessarily recognizing them as
such." T. David Brent, "Jung's Debt to Kant: The
Transcendental Method and the Structure of Jung's
Psychology" (Ph.D. Dissertation, University of
Chicago, 1977), p. 91.

69
   Jung was, for example, impressed with Sir James
Jean's criticism of Kant's notion of space in his The
Mysterious Universe (1930) in Jung to Professor
Lowenthal, 11 April 1947, Letters, 1:454.

70
   In a letter to a philosophy student, Jung wrote:
"Philosophically I am old-fashioned enough not to have
got beyond Kant. . ." Jung to Arnold Künzli, 4
February 1943, Letters, 1:329.

71
   Jung, CW 8:5.

72
Jung's psychological theory of types, worked out primarily with respect to individuals, is indeed a contribution to the development of perspective thinking. What Jung did not keep so consistently in view, however, are the sociological, socio-cultural and socio-sexual determinants of thought, which elements, one may surmise, were more "unconscious" in Jung's time. In Jung's defense, however, one must admit that his theory of the collective unconscious with its social and historical aspects pushes beyond an individualistic view of experience and thought. A provocative treatment of this issue is Ira Progoff, Jung's Psychology and its Social Meaning, 2nd ed. (New York: Julian Press, 1969), especially Part Two.

73
Jung to Arnold Künzli, 28 February 1943, Letters, 1:332.

74
Jung, CW 9/i:38, and Jung to Max Frischknecht, 7 April 1945, Letters, 1:359.

75
In certain polemical contexts in which Jung wishes to dissociate himself from speculation, philosophical or psychoanalytic, he will speak as if his only concern is with facts, not theory. See Jung to Jolande Jacobi, 13 March 1956, Letters, 2:293.

76
Ian Barbour, Myths, Models, and Paradigms (New York: Harper and Row, 1974), p. 6.

77
Jung, CW 4:124.

78
Jung, CW 8:184.

79
Heuristic utility is indicated in Jung, CW 8:184; Jung expresses the possibility of prediction in a letter to E. A. Bennet, 23 June 1960, Letters, 2:567.

80
Jung, CW 8:22.

81
Barbour, Myths, p. 37.

82
Ibid.

83
Jung, CW 8:29.

84
Ibid., p. 28.

85
Ibid., p. 30.

86

Ibid., p. 31.

87

Ibid., p. 6.

88

Ibid.

89

Jung, CW 8:37.

90

Ibid., p. 30. It would be anachronistic to include in this series of analogies the ancient Chinese notion of the Tao (Jung did not seriously encounter this notion until 1929 or so); yet in many ways it is probably the nearest analogue to Jung's model. See his MDR, p. 208.

91

Ibid., p. 38.

92

See Barbour, Myths, p. 40 for the general point about the source of meaning derivation in scientific terms.

93

Jung, CW 8:18.

94

Ibid., p. 26.

95

Ibid., p. 9.

96

Paul Snyder, Toward One Science (New York: St. Martin's Press, 1978), pp. 71-73.

97

Jung, CW8:219. n. 124.

98

Ibid., p. 172.

99

Jung to Pastor Max Frischknecht, 7 April 1945, Letters, 1:361.

100

Ibid., p. 360.

101

Jung, CW 11:469.

102

Jung, The Visions Seminars, 2 vols. (New York: Spring Publications, 1976), 2:391.

103

Whitehead, Process and Reality, pp. 320, 326-328.

104

Jung, CW 6:527.

105

Jung, CW 8:9.

CHAPTER THREE
THE PHENOMENOLOGICAL-MYTHOLOGICAL THEORY OF RELIGIOUS EXPERIENCE

The theory developed in the preceding chapter does not exhaust either Jung's empirical concerns or his theoretical attempts to explain religious experience. In this chapter we will consider a theory rooted, as the previous one, in the empirically given but making different assumptions about procedure and, further, about what constitutes explanation. This theory I call the phenomenological-mythological. I will attempt to show that while Jung often couches the elements of this theory in the language of the preceding one, hence complicating interpretation, the phenomenological-mythological is a genuine, clearly limnable, and independent theory, hence deserving scholarly attention. Specifically, I will attempt to lay out a theory of religious experience rooted in a quest of the psyche in which an individual subject on the way to its wholeness directly encounters numinous powers. The accent will fall more on the descriptive than on the explanatory and on the mythological than on the abstract-literal.

Jung as Phenomenologist

Here and there throughout his writings Jung speaks of his approach as "phenomenological,"[1] of engaging in "comparative phenomenology of the mind";[2] he entitles one of his essays "The Phenomenology of the Spirit in Fairytales."[3] We may charitably grant him his self-designation and description of his procedure even in the face of the fact that the term "phenomenology" has become almost faddish and as such can hardly be defined as currently employed. In his own mind Jung links it with empirical, non-philosophical investigation: "Our science is phenomenology."[4] His own methodological standpoint is "exclusively phenomenological," which, as he says, "is concerned with occurrences, events, experiences--in a word, with facts."[5] Such phenomenological focus on the concreta of reality is perceptual, pre-predicative. It does not judge an experience or event as existent or nonexistent, true or false. "Its truth is a fact and not a judgment."[6]

Jung cannot be interpreted as drawing on the Husserlian program of phenomenology in any direct way.[7] There are no indications that Jung was acquainted with any of Husserl's writings. There are two or three references to Scheler, but these show no grasp of methodological issues.[8] There are no references to Sartre, Marcel, Merleau-Ponty, or Ricoeur. There are several unflattering allusions to Heidegger and his penchant for neologizing ("crack-pot power words").[9] While there is a reference or two to "intentionality,"[10] there is no methodologically self-reflexive sense of the noetic-noematic correlation so fundamental in the phenomenological philosophy developed by Husserl and his followers.

Rather than locate phenomenology in the unity of a school of philosophy stemming from the vision of a great philosopher, it is possible to look at phenomenology in terms of method. Phenomenology is

self-consciously methodological; and while ultimately
the phenomenological method aims at the intuition of
essence through intentional analysis, as a matter of
fact there is no phenomenological method. Husserl
himself employed various methods or steps in
analysis--bracketing (epoche), reductions at various
levels, free variation, and essential intuition.[11] He
himself distinguished two procedures or reductions:
(1) "phenomenological psychological reductions,"
stemming from the period of Logical Investigations,
wherein an eidetic analysis of the essential
structures of the consciousness-acts of various types
of subjective processes (Erlebnisses) takes place; and
(2) "transcendental phenomenology," the science of
transcendental subjectivity and intersubjectivity.[12]
This distinction is sometimes expressed as a
distinction between the "descriptive" and the
"transcendental." Although Husserl's goal was
transcendental phenomenology, he acknowledged the
possibility of the eidetic analysis of a purely
descriptive phenomenology. It is largely the
descriptive phenomenology which has had the greatest
effect and is the method which was exported beyond
strict philosophical phenomenology to the
phenomenological approach applied in many
disciplines.[13]

Of the transcendental phenomenology Jung is
totally innocent even though he faces a parallel
problem of establishing an objective validity in
subjective consciousness. His concern is the more
general one, however, of the universal validity of
individual awarenesses, discoveries, propensities.
Eidetic analysis, however, finds its place in Jung's
armamentarium: what is the essence of that which

grasps one when one is grasped by certain symbolic material? Jung is not particularly concerned with the act of consciousness intending a particular symbol even though he notes the correlative modification of consciousness; rather, he is concerned with the essence of the terminus of the act. To put it in a more technical fashion, he focuses on the noema of the object, not on the noesis. It is this use of phenomenological method that is found in Scheler, van der Leeuw, Otto, and Eliade in religion and, to the degree that they focus on the description of psychic life, in Freud and Jung.

There are other phenomenological approaches with which Jung has affinity and by which he has been influenced, at least indirectly, viz., Kant, Hegel, and Mach. The epistemological limitation to the phenomena as they appear in and to consciousness that Kant claimed had an enormously important influence on Jung. Though Jung like Kant was willing to postulate things in themselves behind the phenomena—and to this degree they both transcend phenomenology—the noetic restriction to what is in consciousness as phenomena was to all intents and purposes a phenomenological position. We shall concern ourselves later with the more detailed influence of Kant on Jung.

Hegel's influence as a phenomenologist is indirect but real, mediated through Romantic psychology. Jung's individuation process, which we shall consider below, is a phenomenological analysis of the transformation of individual consciousness over time and is a less abstract and less cosmic version of the dialectical process of Hegel's Phenomenology of Spirit.

Oddly enough, the positivist physicist Mach can be

seen as having a type of phenomenology which influenced Jung. The former understood phenomenological physics to be a description and comparison of the phenomena in the various branches of physics and on such basis finally to form the most abstract concepts. Mach also saw as his task the elimination of all metaphysical elements from the discipline of physics.[14] This radical focus on the empirical and the attempted elimination of the metaphysical in the sciences finds its echo in Jung's own self-description as an empiricist.[15] In fact, the term "phenomenology" as Jung used it most probably owed more to Mach and his influence in late nineteenth- and early twentieth-century science than to any other influence.[16] It is arguable, however, that Jung's <u>procedure</u> shows far more the influence of non-positivist phenomenology. In fact, I claim this and shall argue such.

Jung as a Phenomenologist of Symbol and of Symbolic Consciousness

Although Jung, as has been previously claimed, is not a self-conscious phenomenologist a la Husserl and consequently gives little attention to the subjective correlate in a cognitive act, it is nonetheless the case that Jung in a general but indirect way comments on the subjective pole in a symbolic experience. Symbols do not occur except in and to some consciousness or set of conscious acts. While this is a seeming banality, it hides an important truth: consciousness is always correlated with some image-object. Jung's epistemological explanations are often unsatisfactory in that he tends to speak of the <u>contents</u> of the conscious or unconscious psyche and generally speaks in a pre-phenomenological way (a theory of ideas, a quasi-solipsist subject, the passivity of the subject in receiving stimuli--in a word, a container theory of consciousness). While not using the language of intentionality, it is clear that the conscious subject is dynamically and intentively related to its image-objects. For Jung the uncon-scious psyche attracts the conscious subject through the imagery presented to it; yet, paradoxically, the conscious subject's attention gives shape and form to the unconscious impulse thereby allowing it to "image" itself. There seem to be various levels of transactions in any perceptual or imaginative experience.[17]

The kind of consciousness, therefore, which is correlated with Trickster imagery is a different kind from that correlated with Great Mother imagery. Different feelings, values, expectations, perceptions, and judgments attend each. It cannot always be decisively decided whether it is the unconscious or the conscious psyche which takes the lead. Is it, for example, a consciousness-with-a-potential-for-exper-iencing a Trickster which in fact experiences the Trickster, or is it the Trickster potential in the unconscious psyche which creates a receptiveness in the conscious psyche for the Trickster? Or is it both?

The correlation between subjective consciousness and its image-objects (Jung often interprets the relation as a compensatory one), while it cannot be described as strictly intentional in the Husserlian sense, does evince a meaningful connectedness. A is meaningfully connected to B (and conversely) if and only if A senses in B meaning for itself (and conversely).

Symbolic Consciousness

While the preceding section dealt with the correlation of consciousness and its image-objects in general, our concern in this section is with symbolic consciousness in particular. Symbolic consciousness, so Jung is to be interpreted, oriented as it is to symbols, is imaginal, non-literal, willing to grasp things as if they were as they appear, playful, willing to exploit the creative possibilities of a given moment, non-rationalistic, dropping all demands that reality should fit preconceived notions, non-consensual, non-controlling (willing to let what-is appear, "come across"), pregnant with possibilities (a depth is sensed beneath the surface of an experienced image-event), and ultimately responsive to mystery--of beginnings and endings, of presence and absence, of good and evil.

Symbolic consciousness as imaginal does not exist, however, except in relation to a literal, semiotic consciousness. If the latter did not exist, if orientation to three-dimensional reality were impossible, if there were no controls, no limits, no necessities, no strict cause-effect sequences, symbolic consciousness would be inconceivable. If there were no signs, no conventional assignation of meanings, there could be no symbols, no non-conventional discoveries of meanings, since for Jung all existence requires opposition--to be is to be in tension--symbolic consciousness exists only in counterpoint to semiotic consciousness.[18]

Symbolic consciousness is holistic and global. It

is holistic in that all functions of the human psyche
are activated rather than operating with the focused
searchlight of a single function (as in one in whom
the thinking function or intellect is dominant and who
meets most if not all waking experience in an
analytical mood). It is global in that all of what is
experienced is attended to without attempting to
partialize it. Obviously, such attitude can only be
relatively employed, owing to the vagaries of
development and temperament and ultimately to the
finitude which necessitates perspectivity. With
respect to Jung's own program, this means bringing
into play both perceptive and apperceptive, rational
and non-rational functions, both conscious and
unconscious dimensions of psychic functioning whereby
both the subject and object are affirmed to be more
than is known and even knowable.

Symbol as Correlative to Symbolic Consciousness

Having attended to the noetic aspect of the act of
consciousness, we turn now to consider the noematic
correlate, the symbol. We must first situate symbol
among other terms indicating the noematic pole, viz.,
"image," "primordial image," "archetypal image,"
"archetypal model," and "archetype (per se)."

Image

The most general term for the "object" of
phenomenological investigation is "image."
Phenomenologically considered, the psyche is a
structured flow of psychic imagery appearing to a
subject.[19] The flow is relatively punctuated by
discernible images. As used here, "image" is not to
be understood as

the psychic reflection of an external object, but a concept derived from poetic usage, namely, a figure of fancy or fantasy-image, which is related only indirectly to the perception of an external object. This image depends much more on conscious fantasy activity, as the product of such activity it appears more or less abruptly in consciousness, somewhat in the manner of a vision or hallucination but without possessing the morbid traits that are found in a clinical picture.[20]

Further, Jung states that usually there is no "reality-value"[21] which is attached to the image (i.e. is worth noting, or at most, very little in describing or referring to the external world). This, however, can enhance its psychological value.

The inner image is "a complex structure made up of the most varied material from the most varied sources."[22] However, it is not a mere aggregation of elements but is a synthetic unity with its own internal meaning. "The image is a condensed expression of the psychic situation as a whole" and not simply of unconscious contents.[23]

While "image" often suggests a reflection of sensory experience (visual shape), Jung intends the term to refer to any representation (Vorstellung) in the psyche. Any modification of the stream of psychic energy with enough definition to stand out from the stream, even momentarily, is an image. Thus Jung can speak of pain as a psychic image.[24]

Primordial Image[25]

Not all images, however, are the same. Within the

constant flow of psychic imagery, most of which is
relatively unimportant, there appear from time to time
images of a striking nature--those which possess a
strong emotional tone, paradoxical features and
conjoined oppositions, and haunting mystery. Viewed
phenomenologically, these images, feelings, and ideas
"come upon one" unbidden, unexpected, and for the most
part unknown. One cannot understand, hence cannot
manage, the image; neither can one let it go. It
haunts, it teases, it disturbs. Efforts to trace it
to personal history and conscious acquisitions fail.
The image seems to be an alien, a surd, set in the
stream of fantasy. The image is experienced as
arising from a level of psychic functioning
transcending the personal-historical; it belongs to
what Jung calls the objective psyche or the collective
unconscious. Since it is primarily to the primordial
image and not to the personal fantasy image that Jung
devotes his attention, we shall consider the
primordial image or symbol in some detail.

Jung's reference to these images, following
Burckhardt, as primordial images (Urtümliche Bilder or
Urbilder) arose from their often archaic quality; that
is, the images seem to convey an aura of aboriginality
and timelessness. Religious symbolism often
emphasizes the antiquity of tradition or the agedness
of the deity: in illo tempore, the Ancient of Days,
the primordial revelation, the two-million-year-old
man who lives in the heart, etc. Such images reveal a
quality which transcends the personal dynamics and
concerns of a contemporary individual. In dreams and
fantasies, the archaic quality may be only a part of
the image, as in the dream of a twenty-year-old male
college student: "The middle paragraph of a letter

from my friend is written in ancient Gothic script."
Or the archaic quality may be expressed in an ancient
figure incongruously set in a contemporary milieu, as
in the dream of a wealthy matron: "I am giving a
garden party in which an uninvited guest appears--a
Neanderthal man."

A high degree of emotionality is often present; in
fact, a mysterious quality pervades the image,
daunting and fascinating simultaneously. The one
experiencing such an image--be it in fantasy, dream,
vision, or hallucination--feels involved to the
utmost; it is inescapably important to the individual;
he or she cannot remain neutral. The image is
terrifying beyond words or blessedly reassuring, often
at one and the same time. Ecstatic transport and
utter dejection are yoked together; the lake of fire
is a sea of grace.

The primordial image, or symbol, possesses,
consequently, autonomy--one is at its mercy--and power
to influence, control, and even suppress the ego-
personality.[26] The image has an _efficacitas causalis_,
thereby demonstrating its own reality since only that[27]
which works (_was wirkt_) is real (_wirklich_).

A further feature is the typicality of the image:
it is not Grandpa Williams; it is a Wise Old Man, an
embodiment of a typical mode of being. Again, it is
not the landlady who comes on the first of the month
to collect the rent; it is an Amazon or a crone, not
any one woman in particular. The images defy
individualization even though _qua_ images they are
concretizations of the meaning typified. They are
concrete but universal. Closely related is the
regularity of their occurrence: the same or similar
situations seem to constellate or evoke the same or

similar images. Many women undergoing childbirth or challenged to serve unexpectedly as a midwife have reported experiencing an overwhelming presence describable as the Great Mother under one of her many guises.[28]

The final quality to be explicitly noted is their paradoxicality, already indicated above. These images are fascinating and daunting, concrete and universal, ancient and contemporary, old and young (the alchemical Mercurius is a spirit <u>senex et juvenis simul</u>), personally important but impersonally straightforward and graphic in their impact but ambiguous in meaning, and sometimes androgynous.

Archetypal Model

If one wishes to understand the primordial image or symbol, one has to proceed comparatively, looking for family resemblances, regularities, and deviations until something like its "essence" reveals itself; one "sees" what the symbol means, what the pattern or motif hidden in the symbol turns out to be. Thus the motif of the savior can be discerned in and among the symbols (and their incorporation into myths) of the hare, the raven, the coyote, the son of unknown royalty, the god-man, etc. No one symbol or myth would fit every aspect of the motif discerned. The elaboration of this motif results in an archetypal model, which is "constructed" by the investigator on the basis of motif research.[29] For example, it is ascertained that the hero has a miraculous birth but then is beset by difficulties--abandonment and early persecution; that the hero receives a call to undertake a journey or mission; that he experiences trans-"natural" aid of some sort; that against great odds he conquers a seemingly insurmountable foe, thereby winning a great treasure by which he blesses his group upon return home; etc., etc.

Archetype (per se)

Presumably, the intuited essence is the essence of something dynamic, real, efficacious. This "something" is the archetype (per se). It cannot show itself to consciousness except through striking imagery nor can it be understood by the mind except through the construction of a model. Jung's usual procedure is to talk about the archetype (per se) in terms of the preceding theory--postulating a cause to account for an effect, hypothesizing the existence of something to account for the regularity in the data, the archetype as a borderline concept, and the like. I will argue in a later section in this chapter that Jung has to say on phenomenological grounds that one directly intuits or senses the archetype. For the present, however, it is enough to state that the dynamic and meaningful presence in the symbolic material is the archetype (per se).

The Individuation Process

Symbols do not just appear as if they dropped out of nowhere into the consciousness of an individual. On the contrary, they emerge in and are implicates and effectors of the process of the individual's own self-becoming. Jung speaks of this as "the individuation process," which he characterizes as "the central concept of my psychology."[30] The centrality of this notion is corroborated both by the frequency of his use of the term and by the pervasiveness of the notion as the conceptual apparatus on which most of his researches into personality transformation and its expression in religious and mythological symbols and motifs hangs. Furthermore, his doctoral dissertation of 1902 adumbrated it in a rather significant way and his magnum opus of 1955-56 made it the capstone. He further claimed that "the individuation process [is] the central problem of modern psychology,"[31] which can be taken to mean that the major concern of modern individuals and of all those who minister to them psychologically is that of understanding and abetting the process in which each individual comes to know, accept, and then to live out his/her own uniqueness. The centrality of the concept and of the corresponding problem is rooted in what Jung understands to be a natural law: the urge toward self-realization is the strongest, "most ineluctable" urge in every living being.[32]

It is important that the individuation process be defined and its nature understood if we are to see how the phenomenological theory of religious experience is rooted in the psychological transformation of the individual. As noted above, the individuation process is a natural, living process--one which a therapist is powerless to create through suggestion or to thwart. It is a biological process as much as the transition of puberty and the climacteric. It is maturation of the individual, a process present throughout the organic sphere. Jung understands the concern for becoming an individual to be a fundamental and pervasive biological phenomenon since only individuals carry life.

Jung recognizes that the human being is not simply biological but also psychological in a unique way, and this fact is expressed in what individuation means on

the human level. The essence of a human being is to
be understood psychologically. Thus the becoming of
what one always was is primarily a psychological
process. One realizes one's total personality;[33] one
attains to selfhood; all of one's psychological
potentialities are actualized to varying degrees but
in a harmoniously coordinated way.

Psyche on the human level is both unconscious and
conscious. If there is to be a development of the
whole personality, then unconscious as well as
conscious aspects are involved. Individuation for the
human is a synthesizing of conscious and unconscious
components.[34] The synthesizing, however, is not
primarily an act of consciousness, or not of
consciousness alone. The impulse for the
synthesizing, as well as the pattern for doing so come
from one's unconscious wholeness, or self.
Individuation, therefore, is the process aiming toward
a realization of one's unconscious wholeness in
consciousness, a self-conscious experience of the
self. One sees and knows and therefore becomes what
one always was and thus truly is. The goal of the
individuation process as well as its already-mentioned
initiating impulse and pattern is the self, the
archetype of wholeness--and of individuality--within
the psyche. The self is seen to be the origin, the
perduring harmonizing pattern, and the goal of psychic
development. The self is first totally unconscious,
i.e., one's wholeness is not consciously grasped; then
one has glimpses during the course of development of
some _spiritus rector_,[35] that the process harbors hints
of direction, meaning, and purpose; then finally, if
all has gone well, one consciously experiences a self-
certifying wholeness which always has been and thus

is.   One is now oneself as one has always been;   the
difference is consciousness.

Jung distinguishes two types of individuation: an
unconscious natural process of individuation and one
in which consciousness has   intervened.   The former
process,   continuous with the unconscious natural
process whereby living things have always become
themselves, can be seen in the countless generations
of human life in which people have developed and
matured psychologically. This is not to say that such
lives are devoid of lonely struggle,   pain, and
suffering;   rather the accent falls on playing one's
part in the vast round of birth-life-death.   In the
latter type,   the process of maturation is quickened
and enhanced by the conscious involvement in the
process.[36]   One not only develops; one is aware step
by step of the process going on in oneself. With each
act of consciousness and each ensuing increment in
knowledge of oneself, the psychic mix is altered,
realigned, and moved ever nearer internal harmony.

The "artificial" type of individuation, in which
conscious intervention is the distinguishing mark, is
a process of differentiation[37] in which the individual
progressively dis-identifies himself with the
commonalities of the collective world, both conscious
and unconscious.   One more and more is able to
distinguish oneself psychologically from the images
previously introjected from family and culture and
from the images of the collective level of the
unconscious psyche.   Individuation is a "setting
apart" (Besonderung) of individuals from others.[38]
Paradoxically, the more one is differentiated--the
more one's own unique nature emerges--the more one
becomes truly at one with humanity.   One reason for

this is that the uniqueness emerges from and in dialogue with rather than in spite of and in contradiction to, hence alienated from, the collective norms, values, and images. Thus, individuation is <u>not</u> individualism, wherein one's egocentricity is emphasized by one's conscious flouting of the collective values, expectations, and obligations: one prides oneself on, and defines oneself through, being different; one scorns the wisdom and value of the collective, both historical and contemporary; one overvalue's one's own perspective, powers, and sense of what is important; one takes one's clues for action from one's own conscious psyche and its values and in so doing represses the unconscious psychic values, hints, perceptions, and judgments. Accordingly, one suffers from hubris and its consequential alienation.[39] In individuation one draws the world to oneself; or better, one draws nearer to the world in that one can precipitate out one's self from the collective only by valuing it enough to take it seriously.

Furthermore, individuation is not the pursuit of Renaissance well-roundedness since such an ideal is a value chosen by the conscious mind of what it thinks to be important. Such orientation, while it may understand the need for the development of diverse abilities, largely follows what tradition or society has judged to be worthy for one. Also there is no guidance as to how much or in what order and ranking the development of each capacity is needed (an equal development of all, if such were even possible, is too conscious and too rational a goal to satisfy one's own living, partly conscious, partly unconscious nature). Moreover, one does not <u>know</u> what and how much suffering, sin, and evil are needed for one's own self-becoming. This would almost universally be overlooked by those pursuing the goal of well-roundedness. It is only slowly and through much experience, much of it painful suffering, that one comes to realize what one is really about and thus who one is.

Nor is individuation a flight from social responsibility since what is discovered in oneself is, among other things, one's social obligations, one's vocation among one's fellows, one's potential contributions and possible legacy. What is often overlooked but is perhaps an even more socially beneficial feature is that in the end one comes to assume one's own responsibility for one's share in the evil of the world, thereby relieving one's environment from having to shoulder unjustly one's own unadmitted evil.

It is not pertinent to this essay to plot the stages or contours of the individuation process. In general, one must move from a stage of unconscious wholeness into a further differentiation of con-sciousness from unconsciousness to a state of conscious awareness of one's wholeness.[40] This entails at a minimum coming to grips with both outer and inner demands, consciousness and unconsciousness, good and evil, first and second halves of life. Usually this is spread out over a normal life span, but in some cases the process is speeded up and a "whole life" is lived in a few short years.

The "coming to grips" is not satisfactorily achieved simply by tacking one thing on to another or by varying one's activities, interests, or values; rather, there must be a synthesis of the opposites. This can occur only when the conscious opposites, pulled apart as far as possible, are resolved through a reconciling symbol, a gift of the unconscious psyche. The reconciling symbol unites the values of both opposing poles in a way that is not rationally predictable; it is literally a _novum_, and the new thing is sensed as being the best possible expression at the moment of where the life line is leading.[41]

The symbol, therefore, is simultaneously the creature and the creator of the individuation process. The symbol transforms the psychic energies into more effective channels as well as being the expression of those energies. The symbol is the _sine qua non_ of psychic development.

The Individuation Process
Phenomenologically Grounded

The tenor of the preceding discussion might suggest perhaps that Jung's understanding of the individuation process is a categoreal necessity deduced from Aristotelian natural philosophy, medieval scholasticism or Leibniz in metaphysics with the concern for the _principium individuationis_, or from a hasty reading of Edward von Hartmann's _Philosophy of the Unconscious_. It cannot be denied that Jung read widely if not systematically in the history of ideas; nor, further, can it be denied that Jung had a penchant for speculation; nor, finally, can it be argued that science neither can nor should hypothesize and in so doing make use of concepts ready-to-hand. However, Jung attempted to ground his concept in oft-repeated observations of the teleological transformation of the human psyche--primarily in himself and in his patients and then corroboratively in mythology, alchemy, religion, and in the social and cultural developments of his day.   In this sense the individuation   . process   is   phenomenologically investigated and founded.

In the first place, the accent falls on the description of psychic events and states rather than on explanation.[42]   He observes in himself and in some of his patients a teleologically oriented process of development.   Like William James and the American pragmatists Jung accepts   tendency,   relation, vectoriality,   and   futurity as perceptual   data. Teleology   is   not   an   alien   interpretive   schema. Directionality,   "drift,"   meaning-possibility   are realities known through intuition, which for Jung is a perceptive, not an apperceptive, function of the psyche.

The   willingness   to   admit   such   features   as directionality,   tendency,   and the presence of   the future   indicate Jung's sensitivity to the temporality of   things investigated.   He, like James, had been enthusiastic over Bergson's philosophy.[43]   Things   and events   are   in   process   and   therefore   temporally positioned.   Images, feelings, ideas, and perceptions are   living   things and are   not   abstract,   mathema- ticized,   and spatialized entities.   Like all   living things they have a time and take time: they have come from   somewhere (they have a history);   they   manifest themselves (they have or are a present); they are tending toward some goal (they have a future).   A full investigation   of any psychic event or component image would disclose its concrete and thorough temporality.

Jung further accented the goal-orientedness of the psyche.   While   teleology   can   be   a   second-order explanatory   principle,   it   is   rooted   in   a   more primordial   experience   of   the   acting-for-an-end   in psychic imagery. This is best seen in series of images. Careful investigation shows in many cases sequence and direction; later images give answers implicit in earlier ones. There seems, on occasion, to be something like foreshadowing in a narrative: a partial glimpsing of the goal of psychological development is finally replaced by a more central experiencing of this goal in such a way that the former is sensed or felt to be integrally connected with the latter.

Obviously, the phenomenological investigation cannot be done by someone insensitive to psychic realities, for such inquiry is not even possible unless one is sensitive to the flow of psychic currents in oneself. The principle of phenomenological investigation, that only one sufficiently attuned to the phenomena by native gift or discipline, is difficult to apply in psychology, so Jung believed, because everyone thought he/she knew himself/herself: everyone is a self-styled expert in matters of the psyche. In addition, the kind of data that the psyche produces is, on the whole, subtle, shy, and ambiguous. A heavy-handed approach or one lacking in either patience or nuance destroys any hope of learning anything (logos) about the human soul (psyche). Unless one genuinely grants autonomy to psychic imagery and processes, one succumbs either to a rationalistic-materialistic view (psyche is "nothing but" consciousness, or "nothing but" brain physiology) or to a spiritualizing one (any event in the unconscious psyche is a voice from the Other Side, from God, etc.).

The investigator must bracket metaphysical assumptions about psychic imagery and claim no more than that there is a seeming meaningfulness to the individual experiences (patient, analysand, dreamer, etc.) in the emergence of consciousness of symbolic materials, that these symbols show some correlation with the circumstances (sex, phase of life-cycle, instinctual needs, cultural level) of the individual's life, and that they are analogous to other psychic images and imaginative products in history and culture.

Jung's researches into dream series, alchemical texts, religious scriptures and rituals, works of art, and cultural phenomena (e.g., flying saucers) reveal, to him, a surprising fact: the psyche moves to produce images of wholeness expressed in images of the conjunction of opposites (male and female, good and evil, age and youth) and of mandala symbolism (Christian Cross, Tibetan Yantras, Navaho sand-painting). The symbolic picturing of wholeness was accompanied by feelings of integration, peacefulness after much conflict, and a sense of order after a period of chaos. Religious people (in the Western tradition at least) often speak of such experiences as grace. They have simultaneously discovered themselves and that which harmonizes themselves. They report having a new center, of being freed from an ego-perspective, of enlightenment.

The phenomenological investigation of the symbols of transformation in the individuation process is at the same time the investigation, as much as is empirically possible, of the archetypal background of the psyche. The symbols are expressions of the archetypes and as such link the fundamental patterns and powers of the collective psyche with the individual. The symbols occupying the metaxic realm

between the conscious and unconscious serve as
mediators between what is most collective and trans-
individual with what is most individual and unique.

Precisely what is mediated from the collective
unconscious is the dynamism of spirit. In Jung's
psychology the realm of the archetypes is the realm of
spirit. The archetypes are those dominating powers
which grasp an individual consciousness (and, in some
cases, whole cultures) and transform it for better or
worse. Spirit operates in the human psyche but
transcends it. Wherever the psyche is overpowered by
some dynamic idea, presence, urge, there spirit is
present. Since it is a phenomenological fact that the
overpowering and ruling presences are plural, the
spirit world itself must be seen as plural (hence,
Probate spiritūs). To expose oneself to such a world
is no unambiguously positive step (hence, Probate!).
Spirit can be evil as well as good, destructive as
well as creative. the archetypes are bivalent, and
the process they determine or influence is therefore
not unambiguous.[44]

The individuation process is life in, and in
dialogue with, spirit; and the phenomenology of the
individuation process is the phenomenology of the
spirit as manifest in the human psyche.

As such, the phenomenology of the spirit is not
identical with the phenomenology of religion. The
dynamic agencies do not necessarily appear as
religious figures; in fact, in the concrete individuation process an individuant may not explicitly
recognize the process as having much, if anything, to
do with classical religious phenomena. The
individuant's concerns may be more the liberation from
environmental influences (parental, social,

vocational, and the like) and a responsible coming to grips with one's instinctual or drive nature (love and sexuality, power, creativity, and the like). Generally, however, if all goes well, the individuant ultimately, through the imagery of wholeness, encounters the archetype of order and wholeness, the self. Psychic integrity is seen to be not only the goal but the source and guiding spirit as well. The experience of the self may be cloaked in traditional religious imagery, or it may not.

Phenomenological Approach to Religious Experience: The Numinous

Our concern so far has been to examine the phenomenological approach to symbols and to the individuation process, the former as the agents and directors and representations of self-becoming and the latter as the matrix of the emergence of symbolic materialism in an individual: life. It remains to be seen how both pertain to religious experience. It is obvious that not all symbolic imagery need be interpreted religiously. Moreover, the individuation process need not be given a religious interpretation. However, both of these elements are central to Jung's phenomenological theory of religious experience. The third aspect to be considered is Jung's notion of numinosity. Religious experience is identical with numinous experience, and numinous experience is connected both with symbols and with the individuation process. But the numinous cannot be with the individuation process. But the numinous cannot be facilely identified with the symbolic; neither can the individuation process be considered as simply numinous either in whole or part. We must turn now to our investigation of numinosity in Jung's writings.

Jung borrows the term from Rudolf Otto's <u>Das Heilige</u>, which was published in 1917. It is not known when Jung read the book or at least familiarized himself with its central concept, but around 1934 the term began appearing in Jung's writings for the first time.[45] He made important use of it in the Terry Lectures of 1937, and increasingly thereafter Jung employed the term. It will be important to discover, if we can, whether Jung simply used the suggestive language of Otto to express his already-worked-out ideas, or whether there was sufficient enough encounter with Otto's notion to alter perceptibly what Jung thought about religious experience. I shall argue the latter alternative.

Prior to the 1930's Jung largely spoke of religion as having to do with the highest value in the psyche, whatever the content:

> When a problem is grasped as a
> religious one, it means, psychologically,
> that it is seen as something very important,
> of particular value, something that concerns
> the whole man, and hence also the unconscious
> (the realm of the gods, the other world,
> etc.).[46]

This would allow us to interpret Jung's theory of religion as an orientation toward the ideal and the whole, whether this be an evolutionary idealism, a monistic idealism, or possibly a pluralistic system of ideal ends: and his theory of religious experience would correspondingly be the experience of the ideals, their lures, and the nisus toward them.

Jung's thinking, however, has always been more dialectical in that while he has emphasized the ultimate unity it is unity only as a synthesis of sharply differentiated noetic and moral opposites. For example, Jung early struggled with the dark God,[47] the God who willed evil,[48] with Yahweh's destructiveness as well as creativeness as seen in the book of Job.[49] Also Jung early saw Christ, who expressed the libido supremely, as connected with the Antichrist.[50] Later his Septem Sermones ad Mortuum would continue his sharp opposition of positive and negative, divine and demonic, good and evil. There is no sense at all that the notions of importance and value exclude the negative; in fact, they require it. Therefore, Jung comes to the reading of Otto not as an undialectical idealist but as one for whom the dualities of existence, the "ambitendency" of the libido, are realities.[51]

In his massive The Discovery of the Unconscious Henri Ellenberger rightly points out the importance of Rudolf Otto's Das Heilige for Jung's psychology of religion. Ellenberger states that the publication of this book "instigated a new direction in the development of Jung's ideas."[52] I consider Ellenberger's historical interpretation reasonable since from 1934 on Otto's terminology, especially "numinous," "numinosum," and "tremendum," appears with frequency whenever religious and archetypal matters are discussed and since he described the shaking effect of the archetypes in ways that showed close acquaintance with Otto: "Numinous experience elevates and humiliates simultaneously."[53]

Ellenberger sees Jung as extending the meaning and application of the term "numinous." Contrary to Otto, who, as Ellenberger interprets him, restricted the numinous to an extraordinary experience undergone by

the religiously gifted--prophets, mystics, and
founders--Jung understood the archetypes as having
numinous quality, and presumably the archetypes are
universal. In the first place, Otto is not nearly so
exclusivistic or aristocratic as Ellenberger makes
him, nor is Jung quite so inclusivistic and democratic
as Ellenberger implies.[54] Both Jung and Otto
recognize that the experience of the mysterium
tremendum cannot be will or manufactured, and that
while it receives classic expression among the
religiously extraordinary persons, it is not confined
to them.

While Otto may have had a catalyzing effect, Jung
had been prepared for the reception of Otto by his own
willingness to work with the non-rational aspects of
myths and symbols, with the androgynous, and the
bivalent. However, after Otto (again it is not clear
how much of this is coincidence, an internal
development of Jung's own thinking, the result of his
own personal development, or what not) Jung more
feelingly roots the paradoxical in experience and not
just in ideation.[55] The numinous is an experience
which the individual undergoes and not simply the non-
rational quality of dream-thoughts and mythologems.
The numen or the object present in or to the numinous
state of mind is experienced as a powerful and
meaning-filled other. It transcends conscious
intention and control. It must be suffered in all its
utter paradoxicality with little hope of rational
comprehension. Jung is increasingly willing as a
consequence to speak of the mystery of the psyche and
of its transcendence at the profoundest level of moral
qualities and judgments.

Both Jung and Otto share a common background in

Kant. However, Jung makes immanent what for Otto is transcendent. It is the archetypes with the objective psyche or collective unconscious which possess the numinous quality; while for Otto the numinous is a quality of the Creator as experienced by humans. This is a metaphysical point of some importance. Jung could not have accepted Otto's reading without recasting it into a less theological, more critical-epistemological mold. We shall examine later whether or not Jung's recasting is ultimately satisfactory.

The Numinous in Psychology and Religion
and Later Letters

Let us examine Jung's first extensive use of the numinous in religious experience, the 1937 Terry Lectures at Yale. The discussion of religious experience is set in the context of his use of "religion" as, following its Latin derivation,

> a careful and scrupulous observation of what
> Rudolf Otto aptly termed the numinosum, this
> is a dynamic agency or effect not caused by
> an arbitrary act of will. On the contrary,
> it seizes and controls the human subject, who
> is always rather its victim than its creator.
> The numinosum--whatever its cause may be--is
> an experience of the subject independent of
> his will. At all events, religious teaching
> as well as the consensus gentium always and
> everywhere explains this experience as being
> due to a quality belonging to a visible
> object or the influence of an invisible
> presence that causes a peculiar alteration of
> consciousness. This is, at any rate, the
> general rule.[56]

Further, he characterizes the <u>numinosa</u> as

certain dynamic factors that are conceived as
"powers": spirits, daemons, gods, laws,
ideals, or whatever name man has given to
such factors in his world as he has found
powerful, dangerous, or helpful enough to be
taken into careful consideration, or grand,
beautiful, and meaningful enough to be
devoutly worshipped and loved.[57]

Phenomenologically speaking, numinous experience
(experience of the numen or numinosum) is of some
power or powers in a subject's world or field of
experience which because of their dynamic agecy and
autonomy captivate and even victimize the subject. It
is experienced as indefeasibly other and as emanating
either from a physical object (quality) or an
invisible presence (effect). The numinous demands
either a careful consideration (the mind is forced,
compelled to turn and return to the object in
contemplation and in circumspect action) or devout
love and worship (the heart, enrapt, gives itself to
the numinous object). This distinction, common enough
in the history of religion, is crucial for Jung in
that it allowed for analytical psychology, a science,
to be one mode of apprehension of the numinous and at
the same time to distinguish it from the more
devotional mode of the churches. Thus, he can quote
with approval William James' remark about the
creedless scientist whose "temper is devout."[58]

In the first place, the experience is of dynamic
factors, doers and effect-makers, "powers." They can
be thematized variously--in personal and non-personal
imagery and in concepts. The experiential root,
however, is pre-rational <u>power</u>. Compare a similar

statement from Otto:

> Before the "gods" were the hard-outlined,
> clear-featured gods of the myths, they were
> numina, and, though the numen certainly gains
> something from subsequent mythology in
> definiteness and fixity of representation, it
> also certainly loses something of its
> original wealth of meaning in the process.[59]

Such power, however, is not simply neutral with
respect to its interpretation. The power in a given
experience is oriented toward the existence of the
subject: it is existentially challenging. That is,
the meaning of one's existence is thereby called into
question. The experienced power or danger is to a
more or less conscious ego pursuing its own goals.
One is compelled not only to note the challenge--as if
it could be avoided!--but also to consider what change
it demands of the subject. This implies that the
powers have in some significant sense meaning and
goal-orientedness. They are not experienced as brute
facts, irrational surds, but as mysterious powers with
something like intentionality. They cannot be ignored
with impunity. They evoke in the subject a sense of
being overwhelmed, evoking awe, gratitude, worship,
and love. Whatever they are, they are not experienced
as less than the conscious subject in meaning and
power, and because of their autonomy they are
experienced as more meaningful and powerful.

Jung recognizes that even the symbolic imagery so
prominent in religious ideation is a secondary
phenomenon. The imagination is stimulated, even
captivated, by the presence of the numen. The numen
is a creative agent and the imagination, at least in
the first moment, is a receptive patient.

Derivativeness is true of concepts <u>a fortiori</u>. The criterion for judging the presence and effect of the numen cannot be derived from some more fundamental source than the numen itself. The numen is trans-rational, if not a-rational or irrational. There can be no valid rational criterion for judging the numen. As Jung puts it: "Religious experience is absolute; it cannot be disputed."[60]

Nevertheless, some assessment will be, and seemingly must be, made by those experiencing the numinous powers. From the psychological point of view, the only conceivable criterion is pragmatic or existential. The experience of a "power" or "presence" and the life based thereon is valid if, but only if, it helps one to live. As Jung puts it:

No one can know what the ultimate things are:
We must therefore take them as we experience
them. And if such experience helps to make
life healthier, more beautiful, more complete
and more satisfactory to yourself and to
those you love, you may safely say: This was
the grace of God.[61]

Elsewhere Jung expresses his "existential pragmatism":

Life is a touchstone for the truth of the
spirit. Spirit that drags a man away from
life, seeking fulfillment only in itself, is
a false spirit. . . . Life and spirit are
two powers or necessities between which man
is placed. Spirit gives meaning to his life,
and the possibilities of its greater
development. But life is essential to
spirit, since its truth is nothing if it
cannot live.[62]

Finally, it is to be noted that for all his

treatment of religious experience, his analysis of dreams of patients which reveal religious concerns, and his interest in the Catholic teaching regarding the dreams sent by God (somnia a Deo missa), Jung does not think this proves any transcendental truth,[63] only, rather, the existence of an archetypal God-image or God within,[64] which is all that can be claimed scientifically. Nevertheless, he thinks this is a "noteworthy fact for any theologia naturalis."[65] As a psychologist, he is not interested in what, if anything, lies beyond the psyche. This is only an honest self-limitation on the part of the scientist, but it must be noted that Jung also increasingly shows how his findings are relevant to the religious traditions, particularly Christianity. It is a peculiar scientific attitude which goes out of its way to share insights with an institution which makes explicit claims about the transcendent, which Jung feels are scientifically inadmissible. His ambivalence is expressed in his saying "there would seem to be good reasons for thinking that even the Boundless (das Grenzenlose) is pervaded by psychic laws, which no man invented, but one of which he has 'gnosis' in the symbolism of Christian dogma."[66] The question here is not whether there is, prior to human willing and doing, a transcendental reality ("The Boundless")--he accepts it--but whether this reality is pervaded by patterns amenable to ˙psychological investigation. Jung makes a "good reasons" case for affirming it.

The influence of Otto continued. We find Jung after 1937--even up to his last writing in 1961-- referring to the archetypes as numina and their effects as numinous; in fact, the link between the

archetype and numinosity was indissolubly forged. The[67]
numinous factors are constituents of the psyche;
from the perspective of the ego they function
ambivalently--sometimes positively, sometimes
negatively;[68] they are paradoxical;[69] they are
powers;[70] they manifest emotional energy;[71] they are
autonomous;[72] they are linked to healing effects.[73]

In fact, the numinous becomes the main focus of
Jung's therapeutic concern:

> It has always seemed to me as if the real
> milestones were certain symbolic events
> characterized by a strong emotional tone. . . .
> The main interest of my work is not concerned with
> treatment of neuroses but rather with the approach
> to the numinous. But the fact is that the
> approach to the numinous is the real therapy, and
> inasmuch as you attain to the numinous experiences
> you are released from the curse of pathology.
> Even the very disease takes a numinous
> character.[74]

The problem in therapy and in living in general is to
become aware when and to what degree "we are . . . in
a numinous situation, surrounded on all sides by
God."[75] It is then that patients, therapists, and
individuants have to learn "to put [their] trust in
the higher powers."[76] In language reminiscent of Otto
and surprising for a major twentieth-century
psychologist, Jung speaks of holiness in relation to
the revelatory power of archetypal imagery:

> Holiness means that an idea or thing
> possesses the highest value, and that in the
> presence of this value men are, so to speak,
> struck dumb. Holiness is also revelatory:
> it is the illuminative power emanating from

an archetypal figure. Nobody ever feels himself as the subject of such a process, but always as its object. He does not perceive holiness, it takes him captive and overwhelms him; nor does he behold it in a revelation, it reveals itself to him, and he cannot even boast that he has understood it properly. Everything happens apparently outside the sphere of his will. . .[77]

At this point it is important to consider a late treatment of Jung's theory of religious experience. He wrote a lengthy letter to a Swiss Reformed pastor who had asked him about the then-bandied-about "religiousless Christianity," popularized by Bonhoeffer and his followers. For Jung this was an occasion for dealing somewhat in detail with religion, an attitude previously defined as the "careful consideration of the numina" (sorgfältige Berucksichtigung der numina).[78] This attitude entails giving serious consideration to whatever numinous experiences--feelings, images, ideas,[79] intuitions, events--which come one's way, elaborating, objectifying in word, paint, stone, dance, music, interacting with--in a word, submitting to--the numinous factors. This attitude contrasts itself with belief (Glaube) or credence (Konfession) which professes a collective faith and specifies a style of living (ethos and behavior).[80]

The individual identifies himself or herself with the group and defines his or her own experience in terms of the group norm. Since the numina are reflected in the mythos and cultus of the community, the individual can have a certain commerce with numina specified; and, for many--in fact for most people throughout history--such an attitude has on the whole sufficed. The normative religious experience is thus communal, liturgical, and sacramental. However, this attitude does not suffice for all, and for many reasons, another approach is more and more demanded by men and women of the present, a chief reason being that the confessional approach stresses, expects, and demands faith (Glaube) which infallibly constellates the opposite attitude of unbelief (Unglaube) or doubt (Zweifel), at least unconsciously.[81] This creates a tension in the psyche of the individual mind: to remain confessionally loyal to the community, which is a condition for remaining within the community, entails the repression of doubt. Such individuals become belief-fatigued (glaubensmüde), neurotic, or find that they simply must revolt in the name of psychic integrity.

Jung sees another alternative, viz., the attitude of religion without creed (Konfessionslose Religion) by which is meant the individualistic (non-collective and non-organized) exercise of the "religious function." This attitude is "the allegiance, surrender, or submission to a supraordinate factor or to a 'convincing' [overpowering!] principle: religio erga principium."[82] The element of power is central in Jung's understanding of religio as a careful account-taking, which implies cautious reserve and the critical use of intelligence. The exercise of careful consideration, however, is possible if and only if the supraordinate factor is manifesting itself. Such exercise is a moment in, and constituent of, an intelligent response to the overpowering factor or principle.

Status of the Archetype

So far we have dealt with Jung as a phenomenologist, with his phenomenology of symbols, of the individuation process, and of the numinous experience. It is important to see what, if anything, the experiential status of the archetype is. It has become clear that for Jung the numinous experience is the experience of archetypal imagery. In what sense, if any, is the archetype itself apprehended? The making out of a <u>phenomenological</u> theory of religious experience requires that the archetype be apprehended.

Jung's language suggests a link between the archetype and the archetypal expression; this, however, does not provide a basis for argument that there is an ontological connection. Furthermore, Jung's scientific-psychological theory could only postulate the existence of the archetype which, as a theoretical construct, is necessarily beyond experience. On the one hand, Jung often speaks from a scientific-psychological viewpoint and in so doing makes the archetype itself an inferential object; on the other hand, he speaks of the archetype itself as acting on a subject,[83] as becoming conscious,[84] etc., so that the archetype is ostensibly a matter of experience.

If Jung is to understand himself and to be understood by others as a phenomenologist, then it must be possible for him in a significant sense to speak of experiencing the archetype. This again raises the issue of Jung's ambiguity as a phenomenologist. If he is to understand phenomenology in a positivistic, quasi-Machian sense, i.e., a simple description of the scientific object, then presumably he can set this activity within a more comprehensive

explanatory framework, which he does with a
scientific-theoretical Kantianism.[85] If, however, he
is to understand phenomenology in terms of what he
actually does, especially in his phenomenology of the
numinous experience, then he cannot exclude the
archetype from experience since the goal is to
experience and describe what is in one's
phenomenological field: The object is given in the
phenomena as the phenomena. The question of what is
behind the phenomena (noumena?) is meaningless. If
one is proceeding scientifically, as Jung also claimed
to do, the focus is on explaining the phenomena by
appealing to principles and entities which are not
observable. By repeatedly calling himself an
empiricist, Jung glossed over the important difference
between the two disciplines of science and
phenomenology.

Jung is victimized by an epistemological
confusion: he tends to think that the archetypal
image or symbol is immediately experienced and what is
not immediately experienced--the archetype itself--has
to be inferred. He fails to distinguish between
immediate experience and direct experience, as he
ought, thereby making it extremely difficult to
maintain an epistemological realism, which, on the
whole, he wanted to do.[86] Just as one directly
encounters one's friend through the mediation of the
friend's face, so one directly encounters the
archetype through the mediation of the immediately
perceived archetypal image or symbol in the psyche.
Calling realism into question, as Jung's language
unfortunately suggests,[87] prevents him from adequately
accounting for the one thing he most wants to explain:
the direct healing power of the symbol. What Jung's

language, and arguably his intention, admitted, but what his "official" theory could not permit, was that the object--the archetype itself--is given in and through the imagery of consciousness.

If we distinguish the scientific theory from the phenomenological on the basis of whether the archetype is given (as in the latter) rather than inferred (as in the former), we still must raise the question of how the object is given: is the archetype (1) directly and immediately given, (2) directly and mediately given, (3) indirectly and immediately given or (4) indirectly and mediately given? I have already criticized Jung for failing to distinguish "direct" and "immediate" and for identifying indirectness and inference. It is logically contradictory to speak of an object as being given indirectly but immediately; thus, we can rule out this alternative. Similarly, we may rule out an object as given directly and immediately since the epistemology implied, viz., some form of naive realism, is notoriously difficult to defend and therefore dubious. Such an extreme realism would seemingly obviate the role of human imagination in the interpretation of experience. Jung tends to speak of what is perceived as existing outside the psyche as mediated necessarily through the psyche--the external object is mediately perceived through a psychic image--while what is experienced as intra-psychic (e.g., a dream figure) is immediate.

The emphasis on givenness suggests the appropriateness of the epistemological language of directness, or, rather, a directness-indirectness axis. Jung's epistemological-linguistic preference is for immediacy, or, rather, an immediacy-mediacy axis. These linguistic distinctions suggest two different epistemological traditions. The first suggests epistemological realism; experience as encounter; interaction between subject and object; fallibilism as opposed to a search for certainty; contextualism rather than foundationalism; presentation of evidence; publicity and openness of experience; historicality; a funded, repeated encounter with what is there to be experienced. On this model the self or subject does not exist or emerge independently of an object or world of objects; subject and object are co-constituted; consciousness is worldly; subjecthood is a cosmological feature. There is a tendency toward empiricism and, in Jung's scheme, toward extraversion.

The second suggests epistemological idealism; dualism; experience as an affair of interiority and privacy; transcendentalism; the subject as trans-worldly, independent and prior to experience; ahistoricality; self-reflexivity; foundationalism and absolutism; fascination with the forms and conditions of the appearance of objects; and conditions of the appearance of objects; representationalism. The tendency is toward rationalism and, in Jung's thought, toward introversion. Whatever is beyond the psychic subject is less than certain. It is clear that different features of the cosmos are better explained by one theory than by the other.

With respect to the phenomenological approach, the language of directness is the more useful of the two. The phenomenological is given, always, immediately in the adoption of a certain perspective if nowhere else. In reality, however, memory and expectation mediate the object experienced as well as does the situation-- physical, psychological, historical, cultural, developmental, spiritual--of the experiencer. The language of immediacy is inadequate for dealing with the phenomenological presentness of the other to the self. Futhermore, the anxiety in immediacy over the certainty of evidence and the need to require such as a foundation for epistemological constructions is alien to the radical historicality and finitude of subjectivity. All experience is necessarily mediate.

Therefore, if Jung as a phenomenologist rejects the immediacy model and situates himself on the directness-indirectness continuum, what are his options? Two possibilities present themselves (I have rejected the two other possibilities in a preceding paragraph) with respect to the phenomenological givenness of the archetype to consciousness; he can adopt (1) a mediated directness of the archetype's presentness or (2) a mediated indirectness. The former can be constructed from his own theory of intuition; the latter can be interpreted in terms of a theory of appresentation, which is based in the phenomenological literature. We shall consider the latter alternative first.

The Phenomenological Theory of Appresentation

The notion appresentation has been developed primarily in the work of Edmund Husserl, elaborated in the social phenomenology of Alfred Schutz and, more recently, given theological application in Edward Farley's Ecclesial Man; and it is the last-named which will supply the exposition and interpretation of Husserl and Schutz. Farley sees Husserl's most important epistemological insight to be that objects directly presented to a perceiver always include appresented elements or references.[88] Thus, any apprehension of reality has a double structure: (a)

presentation, in which some content is directly
intuited, and (b) appresentation, in which a perceiver
grasps some other aspects of an object and its field,
aspects which are co-present. Husserl worked out the
notion first in terms of perceived objects.
Appresentation is Husserl's modification of
apperception, a theme prominent in epistemology from
Leibniz to Kant. The resulting consensus was that
perception (grasping of external matters of fact) and
apperception (grasping of inner states) were two
different modes of consciousness. In Investigations
Husserl abandoned this consensus because it obscured
the way in which apperception is a structural
necessity in perception. Husserl thus modifies
apperception toward appresentation.[89]

For Husserl every act of perception is necessarily
an act of meaning-conferral. To perceive an object is
to intend (i.e., to mean) it as a unity. In his later
writings Husserl was to speak of the unity of the
meant object as a noema, which could be retained
regardless of the empirical fate of the object.
However, the unity and totality of the object is never
directly presented to the perceiver (I don't see the
back of the lamp). Nonetheless, the total lamp, back
as well as front, is given to us in perception through
the mode of apperception or appresentation. We intend
more than we actually see.[90] Through the imaginative
act of filling out we grasp the total object in
appresentation. Farley writes:

> We fill out,in an analogizing act which owes
> its possibility to the imagination, the yet
> un-sensed portions of the object before us.
> These un-sensed portions are not directly
> presented but are appresent. They are

present in the mode of apprence.[91]

Husserl applied the theory of appresentation to
the problem of other minds, acutely problematic for a
transcendental theory of subjectivity, which is
potentially (or latently) solipsistic. In Ideen II
Husserl distinguished between Urpräsenz (which is
originarily or immediately before a perceiver) and
Appräsenz (what is only indirectly present to a
perceiver, or co-present to the directly present).
One's individual temporal flow of consciousness is
present in an originary way (Urpräsenz); such,
however, can never be present to any other subject.
They can only be appresent.

Husserl developed the notion of appresence to
include possible confirmation as the mode of
presentation. This suggests that the appresented is a
hypothesis or a presumption. Husserl is ambiguous:
either the appresented is an inference based on an
analogy to what is presented (Husserl speaks of an
"analogizing transfer"), or the appresented is an
intuition. (Husserl denies explicitly that
appresentation is an inference based on analogy).[92]
Farley himself understands appresentation to be that
act in which we actually intuit components of an
object which are co-present with its directly grasped
facade and which are necessary to meaning or intending
the object as a unity.[93] Farley illustrates this by
the act of perceiving a red ball. One does not
directly intuit its interior. One can only
hypothesize about the specific, non-analytic features
of the interior (is it hollow? solid? etc.) But that
there should be no interior is inconceivable. One
intuits the interior as necessarily co-present to the
directly perceived aspects.[94] The appresented

features are linked a priori to the presented ones.
The grasping of this linking is more akin to intuition
than it is to a hypothesis or inference.[95] Husserl
attempts to apply this to the "ownness" of another: it
is appresented to us through the kind of body and
bodily gestures we know ourselves to be.

A third application of the theory of
appresentation, which is latent in Husserl but
manifest in Schutz, is in the grasping of "background"
realities. In perception the background of an object
now in the foreground is still intended even though
such background is not focused on.[96] This field or
environment is appresented. Farley writes:

Appresentation is that aspect of any
apprehension in which those aspects of the
apprehended object or its field are
"required" by the very nature of that object
but which are not originarily present in the
apprehension itself.[97]

Farley himself wishes to make theological use of the
appresentation of the divine reality with and through
the symbols presented to a community of religious
believers.

The theory of appresentation makes possible an
indirect grasping of realities, and to the degree
perception includes the "unattended to" and as well
the "focused on," the theory of appresentation is
plausible. However, it is not clear what the status
of intuition in the theory (either in Husserl, Schutz,
or in Farley) is. It seems to have only subsidiary
significance. Could intuition be a focal act, or must
it only be the indirect aspect of a directed act of
attention and intention? Furthermore, the intuition
seems to be of a rationalized sort (A ball could not

not have an interior else it would not be a ball). It is hard to see this as an act of perception. One does not normally speak of perceiving the laws of thought though we do "see" them to be valid once we grasp the meaning of the terms.

The assumption behind this theory is that the perceiving self intends (stretches into) a stable, if not static, perceptual object, and intuition is an unfocalized aspect of the conscious act of intending. There is little or no sense on this theory of the object impinging on the subject eliciting or drawing forth the intending.   That is, it is doubtful whether this epistemological paradigm can fit a situation in which the object is dynamically and <u>directly</u> presenting itself to consciousness or where the field or environment is "bearing down upon" the experiencing self.   In this situation the object and its field are directly, even if mediately, presented. Admittedly, the mediation can be a highly complex affair.   The perceiving self is both active and passive, and the perceptual object is both passive and active.   It is doubtful whether the theory of appresentation allows a full epistemological transaction between perceiver and perceived, whether intuition can be a central act as opposed to a peripheral aspect of an act of consciousness, and whether the object of intuition is a specific perceptual entity and not simply a rational content or meaning.

The usage of the term intuition does provide a clue, perhaps, of the way in which the archetype is given to consciousness.   It is possible that Jung's own notion of intuition can provide a useful way of understanding how the archetype is presented to and experienced in and by consciousness.

Jung's Theory of Intuition

In addition to his private valuation of intuition("the noblest gift of man"), [98] Jung made substantial methodological and theoretical use of intuition. Its role in providing hypotheses has come to be accepted in the scientific community even though the exact nature of intuition is debated. To the question whether intuition is simply an inferential process or a sub-species of emotion or feeling, Jung answered in effect, "Neither." Intuition is an autonomous psychic function, and despite the difficulty of the task it can be given a phenomenological description.

Jung observed four basic psychic functions, which became the basis for his widely-known typology. These functions are thinking, feeling, sensation, and intuition. These functions are grouped into rational and irrational; [99] the former judge according to a norm (thinking, according to truth, logical consistency, etc.; feeling, according to beauty, harmony, proportion, fittingness, etc.); the latter (sensation, intuition) perceive rather than judge (evaluate). Thus, in sensation the perceiver simply "takes in" the environment, external or internal, through various sensory-motor capacities. The focus is on the immediately temporally given, the facta bruta of experience. In intuition the perceiver also "takes in" the environment, but it does so in a way that makes no obvious or discoverable use of the senses or of logical inference.

The broadest definition of intuition is perception via the unconscious. That is, one "sees" in a non-sensuous way. One may "see" contemporaneous events (cf. Swedenborg's "seeing" at a forty-mile distance the Stockholm Fire, or a mother's "seeing" her child floundering in deep water only later to learn the child at that moment had nearly drowned). One may "see" past events, at least as they are constituent in present ones. (This is a controversial claim and depends for its intelligibility, let alone its possible truth, upon a philosophical cosmology of events. However, there are certain striking data which suggest such an interpretation as when an "insightful" friend or therapist "sees" in his/her mind's eye a traumatic event, later admitted, in the past of the vis-à-vis). One may "see" future developments, as the destruction of the Holy Place or the captivity of a people. (Also, note Paul Tillich's "seeing" of sheep grazing in the Potsdamerplatz in Berlin a dozen years before it happened.)[100]

Admittedly, this is a complex issue and various interpretative hypotheses are possible and even plausible. Further, according to Jung, whatever is in the unconscious psyche is always possibly contaminated by other contents of the unconscious as well as fused with other functions (intuition, which is perceptual, can be mixed with feeling, which is apperceptual). However, the phenomenological "feel" of certain acts is perceptual, not evaluative. It would only be an interpretation--and a reductive one at that, according to Jung--to explain intuition as, for example, a guess, an unelaborated hypothesis, a judgment about the way things are. Intuition is not a debased or incautious judgment, a confused thought, even though an intuition may serve as the basis for a hypothesis, judgment, or conviction. Furthermore, intuition is not a feeling or an emotion, even though an intuition may be accompanied by and serve as the basis for all kinds of feeling-judgments and affects. Intuition is sui generis. (Incidentally, one of the virtues of Jung's psychology is the unmistakable placing before the educated public of a claim for the autonomous, non-reducible nature of intuition. To deny the irreducibility of intuition now requires argument rather than a dismissal by a wave of the hand.)

Intuition is tha psychic function which allows one to sense the aspects of a thing, event, or situation not available to conscious perception, judgment, or control. It attends to the Whence (background) and Whither (telos) of a thing, aspects which are present in every situation. These two aspects of situations, images, and things are crucial for understanding Jung's notion of the archetype, that dynamic form present in the unconscious which is both the background of an image and also the meaning-possibility present in it. Images, at least the most impressive, challenging, and fascinating ones, are experienced as "back-grounded" and as harboring possibilities for development. They are pregnant with meaning for the self-becoming of the individual; something of import radiates in the image however little it may be consciously and intellectually understood. Such images or symbols impact the conscious awareness of individuals and have their effect on the individual prior to the individual's judgment about their meaning or worth. Thus, both power and meaning are unmistakably present in symbols or archetypal images, which features we naturally take as indicating the presence of something real.

Effectuality and significance are pre-rational, pre-predicative features of what-is. It is intuition which grasps this.

That effectuality and significance attend and irradiate symbolic imagery indicates that the archetypes are mediately experienced. They are also, however, directly encountered. If this were not the case, healing could never take place; there could be nothing strong and meaningful enough to overcome a neurosis, which to the sufferer is both powerful and meaningful, however deplorable, embarrassing, and life-inhibiting it may be. (Neurosis always makes some sense to the neurotic and will be fiercely held onto until a larger sense supervenes. In all psychological conflict--either "natural," as in maturation, or "unnatural," as in illness--meaning struggles with meaning.) It is the testimony of many that healing takes place, that a largeness of life overcomes (overpowers) a smallness of life. This power element suggests the directness of encounter.

It would seem from the foregoing that Jung's theory of intuition better explains the experience of archetypes than the theory of appresentation since intuition allows the archetypes to have a direct, though mediated, effect upon the subject. This would seem to be required if the archetype is to have a healing effect upon the individual; that it in fact is the claim of both those healed from psychological suffering and those who have had conscious religious (numinous) experiences.

Summary

I have attempted to show that Jung has a phenomenological-mythological theory of religious experience, which possesses its own identity and difference from the preceding scientific-psychological theory. On the present theory a person (subject) experiences the archetypes themselves, especially the archetype of wholeness, order, and individuality (the archetype of the self) through archetypal imagery or symbols. The subject directly encounters the archetypes in the symbolic dress; they are not inferred but experienced. The presence of the archetype is signaled by the experience of numinosity, which occurs "in, with, and under" certain symbolic images. The numinous experience is the experience of the archetype, and religious experience is simply the numinous experience. Thus, religious experience is the experience of the archetype(s). Therefore, on the phenomenological-mythological theory of religious experience one encounters in the course of the dialectics of self-becoming (individuation) numinous powers which have a healing and transforming effect upon one. The experience of these powers, especially when ultimately correlated with the experience of the central archetype, the self, is none other than what religious people have always called the "experience of God." As a phenomenologist, Jung need not nor does he wish to say more. The "experience of God" is simply a descriptive term for such numinous encounters. Whether or not the experience of numinosity can be adequately interpreted immanentally and psycho-cosmologically only is a matter for further consideration. Jung made use of Otto, who made pointed theological use of his phenomenological findings. Furthermore, Jung himself has another set of references within his writings suggesting a more transcendental interpretation of religious experience.

Whether this is accidental or is required by the nature of his thought is to be examined. We turn now to a third theory of religious experience to be found within Jung's writings.

1

Jung, CW 11:5.

2

Jung in an interview with J. P. Hodin, 17 June 1952, published in C. G. Jung Speaking, eds. William McGuire and R. F. C. Hull, Bollingen Series 97 (Princeton: Princeton University Press, 1977), p. 220. Jung's modification of "phenomenology" here by "comparative" expresses a theme found elsewhere in his writings: there is no knowledge without the comparison of others within the same taxonomical structure. This, so Jung thought, makes knowledge of the human being and particularly of oneself extremely difficult. MDR, pp. 3-4.

3

Jung, CW 9/i:207-254.

4

Jung, CW 18:289.

5

Jung, CW 11:6.

6

Ibid.

7

Herbert Spiegelberg, Phenomenology in Psychology and Psychiatry (Evanston: Northwestern University Press, 1972), pp. 130-131, notes that, even though two of his former pupils, Ludwig Binswanger and Medard Boss, became quite deeply involved with the phenomenological movement in one way or another Jung had no deep interest in the philosophical movement. The various references to "phenomenology" in Jung's writings are to be taken as communicative devices adopted in response to popular demand.

8

See Jung, CW 9/i:16; 11:516; and Jung to Count Hermann Keyserling, 21 May 1927, Letters, 1:46.

9

Jung, CW 8:171. To a philosophy student Arnold Künzli, Jung wrote: ". . . I hate to see so many young minds infected by Heidegger" (28 February 1943, Letters, 1:332).

10

Jung, CW 5:137, and MDR, pp. 348-49.

11

I draw here on Quentin Lauer, Phenomenology: Its Genesis and Prospect (New York: Harper and Row, 1965), ch. 3 passim.

12

Farley, Ecclesial Man, p. 27.

13
   Ibid.
   14
   I am indebted here to Herbert Spiegelberg's
historical treatment of the modern phenomenological
movement, its precursors, and parallels in The
Phenomenological Movement: A Historical Introduction,
2nd ed., 2 vols. (The Hague: Martinus Nijhoff, 1965),
1:9.
   15
   "Ich bin kein Philosoph [I do not engage in
metaphysics]; sondern ein blosser Empiriker." Jung CW
8:320 (German original); cf. also Jung to Heinrich
Boltze, 13 February 1951, Letters, 2:4.
   16
   An interesting possible influence regarding the
term "phenomenology" is Eduard von Hartmann, whose
seventh edition of Philosophie des Unbewussten (1875)
carried for the first time as the title of its first
(empirical) part Phanomenologie des Unbewussten in
contrast to the title of its second part Metaphysic
des Unbewussten. For the historical facts of its
publication I draw on Spiegelberg, Movement, 1:15.
                    •
   17
   Cf. the following parallel by a contemporary
phenomenologist: "Active attentional focusing does not
create its objects but, as it were, receives them
ready-made from the lower, 'founding,' stratum of the
process in question; and phenomenological analysis is
the process of 'unfolding' these 'layers' of
consciousings." Richard M. Zaner, The Way of
Phenomenology (New York: Western Publishing Company,
1970), p. 171.
   18
   It might be objected that the implicit polarity
of symbolic and semiotic modes of consciousness does
not operate in the so-called "primitive"
consciousness, and that one defining characteristic of
such consciousness is the lack of a semiotic mode; in
a word, "primitives experience the world only
symbolically." This is a "modern" fantasy, no doubt an
updated version of The Myth of the Noble Savage, at
least for those inclined to value the symbolic and to
rue the "modernity" of the modern. So-called
primitives are very well able to orient themselves in
space and time, to develop a rudimentary science, and
to view the world "realistically." The important
questions are: How much? In what circumstances? To
what end? Consider here the claim the cultural
anthropologist Bronislaw Malinowski in his
Magic, Science and Religion, ed. Robert Redfield

(Garden City, New York: Doubleday and Company, 1955), pp. 17-18: "There are no peoples however primitive without religion and magic. Nor are there, it must be added at once, any savage races lacking either in the scientific attitudes or in science, though this lack has been frequently attributed to them.....[A] moment's reflection is sufficient to show that no art or craft however primitive could have been invented or maintained, no organized form of hunting, fishing, tilling, or search for food could be carried out without the careful observation of natural processes and a firm belief in its regularity, without the power of reasoning and without confidence in the power of reason; that is, without the rudiments of science."

19
  Jung, CW 8:325.
20
  Jung, CW 6:442.
21
  Ibid.
22
  Ibid.
23
  Ibid.
24
  Jung, CW 8:353.
25
  I am taking as roughly synonymous "archetypal image," "primordial image," and "symbol." I do so in spite of the fact that Jung attempts to <u>define</u> "primordial image" as a basic form, a mythological motif, which is expressible as a symbol, but he then contrasts it with personal image which is a perceptible form. See CW 6:443-447 for his basic discussion. Is the primordial image perceptible or not? Jung seems to want to say both. Since Jung thought visually and was not terminologically consistent in practice, the interpreter is often at a loss as to what specifically Jung intends. "Image" (<u>Bild</u>) is ambiguous, especially since it is most naturally understood as a perceptual form. Jung himself is to blame for a good bit of the confusion about some of his fundamental notions, particularly "archetype," "archetypal image," and "primordial image." A helpful attempt at clarification is Jolande Jacobi, <u>Complex/Archetype/Symbol</u>, trans. Ralph Manheim, Bollingen Series 57 (New York: Pantheon Books, 1959).
26
  Jung, CW 8:122.

27
Jung's oft-repeated and untranslatable tag is "Wirklich ist was wirkt." Gesammelte Werke, 20 Bande (Olten, Switzerland: Walter-Verlag, 1971), 8:437.

28
See June Singer, Boundaries of the Soul (Garden City, New York: Doubleday and Company, Inc., 1972), pp. 92-93, and Carol Baumann, "Psychological Experiences Connected with Childbirth," in Studien zur analytischen Psychologie C. G. Jungs (Zurich: Rascher & Cie. AG, 1955), pp. 336-370, for fascinating case material.

29
Jung, CW 8:214.

30
Junt, MDR, p. 209.

31
Jung, CW 10:426.

32
Jung, CW 9/i:170.

33
Jung, CW 17:172.

34
Jung, CW 9/i:40.

35
Jung, CW 9/ii:167.

36
Jung, CW 9/i:198.

37
Jung, CW 6:448.

38
Ibid.

39
Jung, CW 8:226.

40
A wider understanding of the individuation process must be distinguished from a narrower one. In the wider, one's whole life from birth to death is seen as a process of becoming who one is--the detaching from the womb, the progressive detachment from parents, cultural norms, and values being part of one's self-becoming. A narrower understanding, and Jung's characteristic position, is primarily a second-half-of-life affair and presupposes a more or less successful adaptation to cultural norms and duties before one can meaningfully--and safely--undertake one's own self-becoming as the central psychological task.

41
Jung, CW 6:474.

42
It is important to emphasize here that (1) the

phenomenological theory, while a theory and thus concerned with explanation, has a "foreground" concern with description and in contrast with other theories seems to be concerned with the "background" (explanation) hardly at all; yet (2) the explanation is largely mythological rather than abstract-literal, implying that this kind of explanation (metaphorical, imaginative) is closer to the descriptive pole than a more intellectualized one. Thus, the personages of dreams (descriptive) are explained as the expressions of the dynamic personal agents, the archetypes, personality being the inclusive category. Furthermore, while there might be a radical discontinuity between the language of description and the language of explanation (e.g., the explosion of an aerosol can tossed into a bonfire is an event observable by the senses and describable in ordinary language which can be explained in abstract terms as volumes of gas, the increased movement of the constituent molecules when heated, the increased pressure against the walls of the container, etc.), this need not be the case at all. The model which leads to a theory also can shape the perception of the data for the theory; the imagination does not only work at the explanatory end.

43
The influence of Bergson on Jung has been inadequately acknowledged both by Jung and by his interpreters. A first step in overcoming this unfortunate state of affairs is the extraordinarily fine paper by P. A. Y. Gunter, "What Jung Learned from Bergson," paper presented at the Conference "Jungian Perspectives on Creativity and the Unconscious," Miami University, Oxford, Ohio, June 2, 1979. This paper appears in a somewhat modified form as "Bergson and Jung," Journal of the History of Ideas 43(October-December 1982):635-652.

44
To speak of dominating, overwhelming powers and agencies as comprising and manifesting from a spirit world "beyond" the psyche is clearly to offer a mythological explanation of psychic events.

45
Jung, CW 8:104.

46
Jung, CW 6:192.

47
Jung, MDR, p. 58.

48
Ibid., p. 38.

49
Jung, Psychology of Unconscious, p. 70.

50

Ibid., p. 230.

51

Jung borrows the term "ambitendancy" from Bleuler, who pointed out that even the most primitive motor impulse is countered by the opposite impulse. Psychology of the Unconscious, p. 194.

52

Henri F. Ellenberger, The Discovery of the Unconscious: The History and Evolution of Dynamic Psychiatry (New York: Basic Books, 1970), p. 723. His historical interpretation is made with Jung's knowledge and, presumably, with his acquiescence. Ellenberger writes that he had known Jung personally, that he had interviewed him on all the obscure points in his teaching, and that he had sent a draft outlining Jung's theories which Jung, after having read it, returned with penciled notations. Ibid., p. xiv. However, Dr. Marie-Louise von Franz, a close collaborator with Jung and probably the most gifted exponent of Jung's ideas, claims that Ellenberger's book "contains quite a few mistakes." C. G. Jung: His Myth in Our Time, trans. William H. Kennedy (New York: C. G. Jung Foundation, 1975), p. 11, n. 10. She does not reveal which points of interpretation she disagrees with.

53

Jung, MDR, p. 154.

54

In some passages Otto is "daunting," as when he says, ". . . whoever knows no such moments [of deeply-felt religious experience] in his experience is requested to read no farther; for it is not easy to discuss questions of religious psychology with one who can recollect the emotions of his adolescence, the discomforts of indigestion, or, say, social feelings, but cannot recall any intrinsically religious feelings. We do not blame such a one." (Rudolf Otto, The Idea of The Holy, trans. John W. Harvey, 2nd ed. [London: Oxford University Press, 1958], p.8). Ellenberger seems to forget, however, that Otto also speaks of the numinous in liturgy, hymnody, the arts, language itself, literature, and in religious experience both "primitive" and "civilized." Jung tends to talk about the numinous in terms of the exploration of the unconscious in therapy, an experience which is obviously not open to all. However, the archetypes are not only available in therapy but in culture and religion generally. Daniel J. Hoy has recently discussed this issue in "Numinous Experiences: Frequent or Rare?" Journal of

Analytical Psychology 28(January 1983):17-32, in which
he claims that Jung defines the numinous experience
narrowly, making it an infrequent occurrence, but he
describes it broadly, making it a frequent happening.
        55
        The assignment of certain historical events as
causes for others must always attempt to avoid post
hoc thinking. Other developments helped to pave the
way for Otto's effect. For example, during the
twenties Jung seemed to be moving away from the
critical focus on the ideational and more toward the
experiential, especially in matters of religion. He
shifts from a more strident agnosticism to a more
sensitive appreciation of the importance of religious
experience, a shift which is seen in the following
revision of an earlier article: "If we leave the idea
of 'divinity' quite out of account and speak only of
'autonomous contents,' we maintain a position that is
intellectually and empirically correct, but we silence
a note which, psychologically, should not be missing.
By using the concept of a divine being, we give apt
expression to the peculiar way in which we experience
the workings of these autonomous contents. . .
Therefore, by affixing the attribute 'divine' to the
workings of the autonomous contents, we are admitting
their relatively superior force. And it is this
superior force which has at all times constrained men
to ponder the inconceivable, and even to impose the
greatest sufferings upon themselves in order to give
these workings their due. It is a force as real as
hunger and the fear of death." CW 7:239 [1928]. Note
that it is the experience which is now seen as the
primary concern: "Science has never discovered any
'God,' epistemological criticism proves the
impossibility of knowing God, but the psyche comes
forward with the assertion of the experience of
God . . . . Only people with a poorly developed sense
of fact, or who are obstinately superstitious, could
deny this truth . . . . The experience of God has
general validity inasmuch as almost everyone knows
approximately what is meant by the term 'experience of
God.'" CW 8:328 [1926]. For the moment, it is not
important to pursue what Jung intends by "experience
of God"; that he accords this important experience
general validity is highly significant and indicates
that Jung is increasingly willing simply to consider
what experience provides. James Heisig, Imago Dei, p.
43, is the source of my understanding on this point.
        56
        Jung, CW 11:7.

120

57
  Ibid., p. 8.
58
  Ibid.
59
  Otto, The Idea of the Holy, p. 198.
60
  Jung, CW 11:104.
61
  Ibid., p. 105.
62
  Jung, CW 8:337.
63
  Jung, CW 11:105.
64
  Ibid., pp. 58, 59.
65
  Ibid.
66
  Ibid., p. 105.
67
  Jung, CW 18:253.
68
  Ibid.
69
  Jung, MDR, p. 154.
70
  Jung, CW 18:707.
71
  Ibid., p. 254.
72
  Jung to Bernhard Lang, 14 Jung 1957, Letters, 2:371.
73
  Jung to Vera von Lier-Schmidt Ernsthausen, 25 April 1952, Letters, 257.
74
  Jung to P. W. Martin, 20 August 1945, Letters, 2:283.
75
  Jung, CW 10:467.
76
  Ibid.
77
  Jung, CW 11:152.
78
  Jung to Eugen Bohler, 14 December 1955, Letters, 2:283.
79
  Jung to Pastor Tanner, 12 February 1959, Letters, 2:484.
80
  Ibid.
81
  Ibid.

82

The original emphasizes the individual character of the response: das Sich Anlehnen, Sich Hingeben, Sich Unterwerfen an einen übergeordneten Faktor. . . C. G. Jung, Briefe, eds. Aniela Jaffé and Gerhard Adler, 3 vols. (Olten, Switzerland: Walter Verlag AG, 1973, 3:228.

83

Jung, MDR, p. 352.

84

Jung, CW 9/i:5.

85

This is the position taken by Roy Uchizono, "Science and Metaphysics in the Psychology of C. G. Jung: An Interpretation" (Ph. D. dissertation, Claremont Graduate School and University Center, 1964).

86

See Richard M. Zaner, The Way of Phenomenology (New York: Western Publishing Company, 1970), pp. 64ff. For a phenomenological critique of the "theory of ideas," which Jung unfortunately bought; and John E. Smith, Experience and God (New York: Oxford University Press, 1968), pp. 21-45 for a trenchant critique of classical British empiricism and for the helpful distinction between directness and immediacy.

87

In this attempt to emphasize the role of the psyche in experience, Jung overstates his case and lands in an epistemological quagmire: "I am fully aware that I am entrapped in the psychic images that we cannot penetrate at all to the essence of things external to ourselves" (CW 8:353); and "[a]ll comprehension and all that is comprehended is in itself psychic, and to that extent we are hopelessly cooped up in an exclusively psychic world" (MDR, p. 352--emphasis added in each of the above statements).

88

Farley, Ecclesial Man, p. 194.

89

Ibid., p. 195.

90

Ibid., p. 196.

91

Ibid.

92

Ibid., p. 198.

93

Ibid., p. 199.

94

Ibid.

122

95

Ibid., p. 200.

96

Ibid., p. 201.

97

Ibid., p. 203.

98

Jung, CW 6:365.

99

"I use this term ['irrational'] not as denoting something _contrary_ to reason, but something _beyond_ reason, something, therefore, not grounded on reason" (emphasis Jung's) CW 6:454. He includes the just-so-ness of nature and of chance under this category.

100

Wilhelm and Marion Pauck, _Paul Tillich: His Life and Thought_ Vol. 1: _Life_ (New York: Harper and Row, Publishers, 1976), pp. 124-25.

CHAPTER FOUR
THE METAPHYSICAL-THEOLOGICAL THEORY OF RELIGIOUS EXPERIENCE

In the previous chapters we have considered two
theories of religious experience implicit in Jung's
work, the scientific-psychological and the
phenomenological-mythological. We now turn to a
third, the metaphysical-theological. It must be
admitted at the outset that the evidence for this
theory is with a few exceptions more circumstantial,
less direct than with the first two. It is the theory
that Jung would least willingly own. Therefore, it
will be the burden of this chapter to argue that the
metaphysical-theological theory is instantiated in
Jung's writings despite Jung's probable demurrals.

The central thesis of such theory can be simply
put: the experience of the numinous archetype,
especially of the central archetype of the self or
God-image, is an experience of God the metaphysical
ultimate. This means that in the experience of
numinosity, spelled out in the preceding theory, one
is encountering directly, even if mediately, "the
transcendent being"[1] or "Being itself."[2] In order
that the hypothetical or interpretive aspect of the
theory may be kept in view, the theory should be taken
as follows: numinous data, well attested in the inner
experience of many people across culture and history

including contemporary experience, are ultimately best explained as the expression in the human psyche of the metaphysical ultimate. This obviously transcends the concerns of the scientist and even of the phenomenologist. Yet it will become apparent that Jung's concerns could not be confined to science and phenomenology; he became a metaphysician/theologian in spite of his professed self-restriction to empirical science. Furthermore, this function had to be engaged in, even implicitly, if his understanding of religious experience is to be fully intelligible. The metaphysical demand for intelligibility is only partially, grudgingly, and ambiguously satisfied by Jung; it is my purpose to spell out his implicit metaphysical-theological theory.

The case for the thesis is to be made both semantically and operationally, i.e., by what Jung said either explicitly or implicitly and what he did. Specifically, I will consider Jung's direct statements, his rhetoric about archetypes, his use of Kant, his use of Rudolf Otto, and his concern with theology and theologians.

Direct Statements in Support of the Thesis

Jung's direct statements about the experience of the numinous archetypes as the experience of God the metaphysical ultimate are few and appear largely in his last decade. In response to a query from a pastor about the relation between the archetypes and God's power, Jung writes: "If one assumes that God affects the psychic background and activates it or actually is it, then the archetypes are, so to speak, organs (tools, Werkzeuge) of God."[3] The context of Jung's answer makes it clear that he has given an elliptical hypothetical argument in which are omitted both the minor premise ("I assume that God affects the psychic background and activates it or actually is it") and the conclusion ("Therefore, the archetypes are organs or tools of God"). Since the archetypes as the organs or tools of God are the media of God's working, are the expression of God's effecting hence effective presence, the experience of the archetypes is a direct even if mediated encounter with God. It is not enough simply to say that one encounters a God-image, which may or may not express the metaphysical ultimate; the God-image is a God-image because it does express the effectivity of the ultimate reality.

Jung again writes to a pastor that "the gods . . . [represent] the numinous aspects of the transcendent being as a plurality."[4] It is obvious here that Jung is linking the experiential and the metaphysical in that numinosity is a quality confidently to be found only in the vital experience of human beings, which quality is pluralistically encountered but which is to be taken as the re-presentation to the experiencing subject of the transcendent being, the ontological One for the experienceable and experienced Many. Jung is not clear--here or anywhere else in his writings--why he feels a need to harmonize an experienced plurality into a metaphysical (non-empirical, non-experiential) One. He notes as an empirical fact that there is an experienced unity or harmony only after a process of experienced plurality: "The ego has to acknowledge many gods before it attains the centre . . ."[5] But why should he take this empirical observation as an analogy of the relationship between the empirical and metaphysical dimensions? Does it rest in a trans-categoreal intuition? He takes it as certain that God is Being itself[6] and that "[t]he existence of a transcendental reality is evident in itself."[7] He writes further: "For me 'God' is a mystery that cannot be unveiled . . ."[8] and ". . . God is the Unfathomable itself."[9] He does not say how the apprehension of either noetic certitude or rationally impenetrable mystery is possible. He only finds that he "must" affirm the reality of the metaphysical ultimate.[10] (In fact, one of the difficulties of Jung's psychology is that he claims to know what cannot be known by his psychology: there is ultimate being.)

Consider further Jung's comments to Sir Herbert Read, one of the editors of the Collected Works and a self-confessed humanist:

> Archetypes are forms of different aspects
> expressing the creative psychic background.
> They are and always have been numinous and
> therefore 'divine.' In a very generalizing
> way we can therefore define them as
> attributes of the creator.[11]

The experienceable archetypes are differentiations or manifestations of the creative ground of the psyche. He does not work out systematically the relationships between "forms," "aspects," and "creative psychic background." Nor does he connect in any satisfactory way the "creative psychic background" and the transcendent being. It is obvious that the psychic background transcends any and all psychic expressions. Whether it transcends all finitude absolutely is not clear. Jung does speak of the unus mundus, the "transcendental psychophysical background," neutral in itself and potential to all actualization.[12] Conceivably, the transcendent being is also the creative ground of the psyche. Jung has

no explicit theory of divine creation nor do his
insights on this matter necessarily cohere.[13] He
seems to leave it as a metaphysical insolubile. Yet
it is to be noted that he asserts that the archetypes
are attributes of the creator, whether conceived as
the transcendent being itself or as the creative
psychic background.

The warrant for taking his expressions about the
experience of numinosity as expressions of a
transcendent being or creator as evidence for a
metaphysical-theological interpretation of religious
experience, the central affirmation of which is that
numinous experience is the experience of God, is, of
course, that Jung's statements, largely from the last
decade of his life and found mainly in his letters,
are to be accorded systematic significance. That is,
letters to pastors are not to be seen as flattering
attempts to win clerical acceptance of his psychology;
nor are the private reflections of a man in conspectu
mortis to be seen as reversals of a reputedly long-
held metaphysical neutralism or agnosticism. Rather,
they are to be seen as explicitations of the
implications of his theoretical and practical work as
well as his own experience.

With respect to the first it must be said that the
tone of Jung's letters is frank, earnest, and
sympathetic, that while he felt his work had enormous
importance for the Church, he was not sanguine about
its easy acceptance nor was he eager to do more
towards its acceptance than to write and to speak
candidly.[14] With respect to the second it can be
shown that there are metaphysical hints throughout his
career,[15] and that while Jung never wishes to engage
in the metaphysical enterprise, he did not deny the

existence of a metaphysical realm or dimension to existence. Yet it would seem that a few direct assertions, as useful as they are, are in themselves not fully persuasive since not all semantic ambiguities can be cleared up. We must look for other evidence if we are to establish solidly the metaphysical-theological theory of religious experience in Jung's writings.

Indirect Evidence in Support of the Thesis: Metaphysical Rhetoric

A second strand in the evidential rope is Jung's metaphysical language regarding the archetypes. Jung heartily wished to avoid having his notion of the archetype interpreted as a metaphysical ens, yet paradoxically he drew on the Western philosophical tradition for his rhetoric about the archetype. While to some degree this can hardly be avoided, most scientists, particularly in a culture shaped by positivism, make a strenuous effort not to label their discoveries with language from Heraclitus, Plato, Augustine, Leibniz, the alchemists, Kant, Schopenhauer, Hegel, and Rickert. No doubt this was due in part to Jung's terminological conservatism; he felt he had a better chance of being understood if he used language familiar to his educated readers. The term "archetype" itself is a case in point, being found in Philo, Irenaeus, the Corpus Hermeticum, Dionysius the Areopagite, and by idea if not by term in Plato and St. Augustine.[16] He speaks of the archetypes in themselves apart from manifestation,[17] in their "innermost essence,"[18] their apriority,[19] their universality,[20] their approximation to oneness and immutability,[21] their determination of all

existence,[22] their essential irrepresentability,[23] and
their "eternality."[24] Consciously or not, he is using
language not only of hoary metaphysical service but
also of meta-empirical import. Jung hoped to settle
the problem by making anti-metaphysical disclaimers,
by trying to distinguish science from metaphysics with
respect to the function and status of statements
(science hypothesizes; metaphysics hypostasizes), and
by his frequent assertion that he was "a mere
empiricist" (ein blosser Empiriker).[25]

He does not seem to see that terms like "essence,"
"things in themselves," "immutability," "eternal,"
"universal," "essential irrepresentability" are
neither necessary to nor useful for empirical
investigation. In fact, in a strictly empirical
science such terms are improper, contravening the
empirical spirit. In partial self-defense Jung wrote:

> Not withstanding the fact that I have often
> een called a philosopher, I am an
> empiricist and adhere to the
> phenomenological standpoint. I trust that
> it does not collide with the principles of
> scientific empiricism if one occasionally
> makes certain reflections which go beyond a
> mere accumulation and classification of
> experience.[26]

That one makes reflections which go beyond the facts
is certainly part of the scientific enterprise.
However, some of Jung's reflections tend to be
expressed in terms suggesting generality of the
highest level and the widest scope of application.
The question arises whether Jung's metaphysical
language is an innocent but unfortunate borrowing from
the philosophical tradition and essentially devoid of

metaphysical import, or whether the metaphysical language necessarily carries some metaphysical freight. In either case, he fails to convince his readers of his proclaimed a-metaphysicalism.

At one level, it would be unfair to deny Jung's empiricism and to interpret any metaphysical language he may have used as anything other than abstract or generalizing language of which any hypothesizing must make use. Jung was clear in his own mind that he was putting forth hypotheses to be tested by other responsible researchers. His commitment to scientific method has been documented above. However, Jung was not only a scientific researcher proffering testable hypotheses for collegial validation or refutation; he was also a man deeply concerned with issues of human transformation, which necessarily entails a concern with values cultural, moral, and religious. He could not avoid the metaphysical dimensions of the transformation of individuals and cultures. The healing power of the archetypes as he witnessed it in himself and others militated against evaluating the archetypes as hypothetical entities, at least exclusively so. The radically self-involving imagery and experiences entail the metaphysical. Therefore, Jung's theory of the archetype willy-nilly takes on a metaphysical aspect when the meaning and value of human transformation are at stake.

Jung's language, especially as he focused on the archetype, revealed two distinct but interrelated functions: explanation and disclosure. The former orients the mind to the world, helping one to make intelligible connection among the parts; one proceeds analytically and discursively. This function has been gloriously fulfilled in modern science. The latter

attempts to show what is, to help one see and in
seeing to become. One proceeds synthetically and
intuitively. This function has been performed by
religion and the arts and now, at least in part, falls
into the province of depth psychology. Transformation
comes through vision, and vision through the interplay
of imaginal structures and movements. What begins as
an explanation in Jung's writing often becomes an
instrument of seeing reality in a certain--and new--
way.

Jung claimed self-consciously to use language
ambiguously. He writes:

> The language I speak must be ambiguous, must
> have two meanings in order to be fair to the
> dual aspect of the psyche's nature. I
> strive quite consciously and deliberately
> for ambiguity of expression, because it is
> superior to singleness of meaning and
> reflects the nature of life. My whole
> temperament inclines me to be very
> unequivocal indeed. That is not difficult,
> but it would be at the cost of truth. I
> purposely allow all the overtones and
> undertones to chime in, because they are
> there while at the same time giving a fuller
> picture of reality. Clarity makes sense
> only in establishing facts, but not in
> interpreting them.[27]

If what Jung writes about his procedure is accurate,
then one--and this includes Jung himself!--should not
be surprised to find that some of his language has
metaphysical vectors as well as scientific ones, that
metaphysical assumptions lurk among his scientific
observations, and that Jung cannot fully control the

interplay of perspectives opened up by his language.

As a case in point--and this is one among many possible citations--Jung comments on the dogma of the Trinity:

> . . . any statements of this kind can--and
> for scientific reason, must--be reduced to
> man and his psychology, since they are
> mental products which cannot be presumed to
> have any metaphysical validity. They are,
> in the first place, projections of psychic
> processes, and nobody knows what they are
> 'in themselves' (was sie 'an sich' sind),
> i.e., if they exist in an unconscious sphere
> inaccessible to man (wenn sie in einen
> unbewussten. . . .Bereiche existieren).[28]

Note that Jung attempts to answer the question about what they essentially are by asking whether they exist somewhere beyond consciousness. Jung is making two assumptions: (1) the Trinity-symbol expresses something which exists in itself, but we do not know what it is; (2) this symbol exists for us (in consciousness), but whether it exists for itself (beyond consciousness) we do not know. The first assumption is metaphysical; the second, scientific. That they are woven together in the same sentence makes unambiguous interpretation almost impossible.

Another way of putting the point is to say that Jung has two views of language operating simultaneously. On the one hand, the development of the scientific world-view has led to an epistemology which sees a chasm between the system of ideas in the mind and reality (Locke's division between nominal essences and real essences is a telling example). This leads to a view of language in which human beings

arbitrarily assign meanings to things, manipulate
verbal counters with little or no confidence that they
are talking about things: language can only
externalize or express the ideas of the mind. This
has led to the crisis of intelligibility. On the
other, the more traditional view and its
repristination in certain contemporary
hermeneuticists, language discloses reality because
reality controls language; the linguistic happening is
the self-manifestation in human speech of what is, and
the attention to what is said is the way into being.[29]
Jung attempts both to explain and to disclose--to
reach out to what is through self-restricted
manipulating and expression of ideas and to let
reality disclose itself through language (let Being
"speak"). Jung in part, therefore, is engaging in
metaphysical rhetoric, and such rhetoric cannot be
scrubbed clean of all metaphysical import.

Jung as an Unconscious Metaphysician

The preceding section attempted to show that
Jung's language in part was metaphysical, especially
as he dealt with the archetypes; in this section I
wish to show that Jung was engaging in metaphysics in
spite of himself. At the conscious level Jung not
only was a-metaphysical but in some moods anti-
metaphysical as well. Consider the following
statements:

> Any honest thinker has to admit the
> insecurity of all metaphysical positions, and
> in particular all creeds. He has also to
> admit the unwarrantable nature of all
> metaphysical assertions and face the fact
> that there is no evidence whatever for the

ability of the human mind to pull itself up
by its own bootstrings, that is, to establish
anything transcendental.[30]

. . . my aim as a psychologist is to dismiss
without mercy the metaphysical claims of all
esoteric teachings. . . . I quite
deliberately bring everything that purports
to be metaphysical into the daylight of
psychological understanding, and do my best
to prevent people from believing in nebulous
power-words. . . . One cannot grasp anything
metaphysically, one can only do so
psychologically. Therefore I strip things of
their metaphysical wrappings in order to make
them objects of psychology.[31]

The preceding statements are perhaps best understood
as polemical overreachings, fired by the encounter
with the charge of psychologism and the seeming need
to believe rather than understand. A more
characteristic expression can be seen in Jung's
response to an American graduate student preparing a
doctoral dissertation on the religious and
philosophical issues between Buber and Jung. He
wrote:

I am sorry if X. bothers about the question
of the basis upon which 'religion rests.'
This is a metaphysical question the solution
of which I do not know. I am concerned with
phenomenal religion, with its observable
facts, to which I try to add a few
psychological observations about basic events
in the collective unconscious, the existence
of which I can prove. Beyond this I know
nothing and I have never made any assertions

about it.

How does Buber know of something he cannot "experience psychologically"? How is such a thing possible at all? If not in the psyche, then where else? You see, it is always the same matter: the complete mis-understanding of the psychological argument: 'God' within the frame of psychology is an autonomous complex, a dynamic image, and that is all psychology is ever able to state. It cannot know more about God. It cannot prove or disprove God's actual existence, but it does know how fallible images in the mind are.[32]

There are at least two reasons why Jung resisted a description of his work in any sense as metaphysical--one tactical, one strategic. First, the tactical reason is that acceptance of metaphysics in the late nineteenth- and early twentieth-century milieu could have jeopardized his scientific undertakings and standing in the scientific community. He admits that as a young scientist he wanted nothing more than to be accepted by his scientific colleagues,[33] an understandable enough motive. Already something of a counter-cultural spirit, Jung feared abandonment by what he saw as the most spiritually advanced group of the time, the scientists. To be branded "metaphysical"--or what was worse, "mystical"--was the kiss of death.

The strategic reason for resisting having his work labeled as metaphysical is Jung's understanding of metaphysics as providing empty knowledge, a "news from nowhere."[34] Transcendent knowledge is spurious, illusory. If a claim lacked empirical rooting, i.e., could neither be verified nor falsified by appeal to experience, then for Jung the claim could never--in principle--be known to be true and thus could not be responsibly asserted. Furthermore, he was convinced by Kant of the antinomies of reason and therefore granted human rationality no superior role in arbitrating competing claims. If anything could make claim to truth, it was experience. Jung understood metaphysics as rootless rationalism, the feeble efforts of a consciousness unconscious of its springs as well as the deeper, non-rational elements in experience. Thus, those who engaged in metaphysics were unaware of their rationalizing of archetypal experience. He saw philosophers acting as if ideas were the creations of their own minds and therefore under their control. He saw them as ignorant of their own dynamic unconscious and its archetypal contents. Cut off from a vital contact with these powerful forces, philosophers could only deal with them after the intellect had sanitized and depotentiated these archetypal energies. Archetypes are then seen as concepts, as rational counters in a giant shell game-- dangerous because the players are duped about their own archetypal determinedness. Unconscious persons, especially if highly rational, are capable of untold evil <u>just because</u> of their unconsciousness. Metaphysics is, therefore, morally dubious.

Jung thinks he is supported in his anti-metaphysicalism by Kant, whom he reads largely as an epistemological idealist. Kant, so read, made it possible for Jung to navigate between the Scylla of theology with its transcendent affirmations and the Charybdis of a materialistic positivism with its transcendent denials. Like Kant and Hume, Jung wanted

to bracket any and all transcendent affirmations.
Unlike Freud and nineteenth-century positivists he did
not wish to reduce transcendent claims simply to
immanent causes, either biological-psychological or
physical. Rather, Jung wished to transcendentalize
transcendent referents, making them the immanent
conditions for the possibility of experiencing and
knowing. If transcendental statements also had
transcendent reference, he neither knew nor needed to
know. At least this was his epistemological reading
of Kant.

Consider a typical "Kantian" appeal by Jung:
Of the essence of things, of absolute being,
we know nothing. But we may experience
various effects: from 'outside' by way of the
senses, from 'inside' by way of imagination.
We would never think of asserting that the
color 'green' had an independent existence,
similarly, we ought never to suppose that an
imaginative experience exists in and for
itself, and is therefore to be taken
literally. It is an expression, an
appearance standing for something unknown but
real.[35]

This statement, however, is Kant, but Kant-plus-
metaphysics; and it is this "more" which troubles the
perceptive reader and which Jung on the whole seems
not to see. Consider the following statement by
Edward Casey, astutely commenting on this passage:
This very Kantian-sounding statement is in
the end quite unKantian. Although Jung is
granting with Kant that we can know
appearances alone (in this case, imaginative
appearances or presentations), he is

asserting, in spite of a stated aversion to metaphysics, that the thing in itself can be characterized as real--that archetypes, as the ultimate metaphysical things in themselves, are metaphysically real because they are capable of producing certain "effects." Yet if Kant is right concerning the noumenal status of things in themselves, then we should not be able to say anything at all about them--not even that they are causally efficacious in some unknown way. In this dispute we must invoke Jung against himself: "Whether we will or no, philosophy keeps breaking through" (CW 7:119). It breaks through this time in the form of Jung's own thesis concerning the metaphysical status of archetypes. For even if the real is to be judged only by its effects, to assert the existence of these effects (as Jung explicitly does) is necessarily to presume the reality of their archetypal cause, and thus to indulge in metaphysics despite Kant's and Jung's own warnings.[36]

Two things, however, need to be said. One, there is evidence aplenty that Kant was engaging in metaphysics malgré lui, contrary to what his largely idealistic, epistemologically oriented, nineteenth-century interpreters believed.[37] Two, Jung gives evidence that while he utilizes Kant primarily for his own epistemological purposes, he is also aware of the metaphysical dimensions in Kant: he acknowledges the Ding an sich to be not simply a negative concept, and he also connects the things in themselves with archetypes, which are "the determinants of all existence,"[38] psychic and non-psychic. With his notion of the transgressivity of the archetype in which the archetype transcends psychic causal efficacy and is able to effect and order physical phenomena as well, Jung has squarely put himself into the role of metaphysical cosmologist. Because he was somewhat tentative about certain of his suggestions, e.g., that whole numbers are archetypes, he could understand himself as not engaging in metaphysics since, as he saw it, metaphysics was dogmatic and essentially aprioristic whereas science had a built-in openness and tentativity. Jung never saw metaphysical speculations by metaphysicians as intentionally hypothetical. (Of course, as a scientist he viewed metaphysical speculations as nothing but hypotheses-- and inadequate ones at that!) Thus, as long as he offered his speculations as tentative he could consider himself as a scientist no matter what the level of abstraction. Jung notwithstanding, to proffer abstract, universally applicable categories, even hypothetically, is to engage in metaphysics.

Jung's Use of Otto

As noted in the previous chapter, Jung made extensive use of some of Rudolf Otto's concepts, especially that of numinosity. It could be argued on Jung's behalf that his use of Otto was highly selective; that he prescinded from a metaphysical interpretation of phenomenological findings, refusing to follow Otto's lead (it is manifestly clear that Otto intended to link his concept of the mysterium tremendum et fascinans with the theological God); and that such limited employment of a thinker's concepts is justifiable: Jung's restricted non-metaphysical utilization of Otto is legitimate.

However, Jung imported far more of Otto than he intended. If, as Jung says, "the term 'god' should only be applied in case of numinous inconceivability,"[39] and if Jung is using language literally and assertorically, then he was in agreement with Otto in placing God beyond any naturalistic framework such as psyche. The reason for this is that a naturalistic system--and a fortiori all its elements--is conceptually determinable, hence conceivable, even if in fact such a system is, at a given moment at least, conceptually indeterminate. Perhaps among the reasons that Jung does not see himself as engaging in metaphysics here is that there is a sense in which the inconceivably numinous is conceivable since one can mark it off linguistically from the non-numinous. This distinction, however, operates on another logical level: the ground of conceivability is not to be compared with one of the conceived or conceivable elements. Generally, however, Jung is interested in res, not verbum, so this possible objection is not to be taken seriously. Therefore, by accepting in so fundamental a manner Otto's language of numinosity, Jung is willy-nilly acknowledging the disclosure of a trans-natural, trans-systemic ground.

Jung's Concern with Theology and Theologians

Despite his early rejection of and continued annoyance at theology, Jung was interested in theology in one way or another all his life. His initial rejection seems in large part to have been based on the non-experiential, rationalistic character of theology of the late nineteenth century. Jung's career can be read as an attempt to provide an experientially-based religious thought to solve a problem that his father and both his father's and his own contemporaries could not. He seemingly worried about the relativization of Jesus in Schweitzer's Quest of the Historical Jesus. He was aware of the work of Barth and Bultmann. He showed great interest in having Victor White, O.P., for a possible collaborator and was greatly disappointed when such collaboration did not work out. He seemed quite interested in the questions which theologians and pastors put to him. While he himself did not wish to make metaphysical assertions, he seemed not unwilling, however, for theological affirmations to be made by theologians on the basis of what he had discovered, notably the archetypal image of the Deity, which owing to its relative frequency in the psychic ees of humankind, including his own patients, "seems to be a noteworthy fact for any theologia naturalis."[40]

Consider the full statement:

It would be a regrettable mistake if anybody should take my observations to be a kind of proof of the existence of God. They prove only the existence of an archetypal image of The Deity (das Verhandensein eines archetypischen Bildes der Gottheit), which to my mind is the most we can assert about God psychologically. But as it is a very important and influential archetype, its rel- atively frequent occurrence seems to be a noteworthy fact for any theologia naturalis. And since the experience of this archetype has the quality of numinosity, often in a very high degree, it comes into the category of religious experiences.[41]

Two observations need to be made. (1) Why should he
care whether or not his findings aided natural
theologians, especially since he was not convinced of
the viability of the proofs for the existence of God?
The contradiction aside, his going out of his way to
point out to theologians how his discoveries could be
used for their purposes bespeaks some concern for, and
some conviction of the legitimacy of, their
enterprise. (2) Where he says that his observations
"prove only the existence of an archetypal image of
the Deity, which to my mind is the most we can assert
psychologically about God," his rhetoric unwittingly,
we may suppose, reveals his own conviction. If he
were metaphysically neutral, most likely, he would not
have said "archetypal image of the Deity" but rather
something like "a god-image," the subjective genitive
of the former suggesting the expression in the psyche
of something real: the Deity. Furthermore, there is
an implied assertion in the phrase "the most we can
assert psychologically about God." Jung could have
said, "an alleged God," "a hypothesized deity," or "a
possible Divine source," or the like. In another
context he gives what is patently a specious argument
when he says that "archetype" etymologically implies
an imprinter.[42] That he even makes the argument
signifies his belief in a metaphysical transcendent;
and, contrary to his intention, he invites the
metaphysicians to see and to explicate his trans-
scientific assumption.

Contrary to his expressed intentions, Jung has
implicitly provided a metaphysical-theological theory
of religious experience. The premise of his
metaphysical conviction makes a two-fold

interpretation of many of his statements necessary: he must be taken as sincerely attempting to restrict himself to empirical investigation and to avoid doing metaphysics and theology, and he must be interpreted as implicitly engaging in these disciplines. Something like this should have been expected by his adoption, on the one hand, of a scientific approach and, on the other, by his attempting simultaneously to include within his "science" of psychology the issues which metaphysics and theology had traditionally considered. Jung thought he could avoid the latter orientation by concerning himself with empirical method; however, substantive concerns continued to break through. Jung was a scientist by choice but a metaphysician malgré lui.

Metaphysics and Jung: A Concluding Note

At the conclusion of this chapter, it is perhaps useful to clarify how I conceive of metaphysics since I am making much of the fact that Jung willy-nilly engages in metaphysics. First of all, metaphysics is to be generally understood as any speculative theory which is abstract, universal in scope, systematic, and specifiable by the particulars of experience.[43] In this sense, metaphysics is neutral between immanent and transcendent accounts of norms, forms, and facts. More specifically, however, I distinguish three levels of trans-empirical speculation: cosmological, metaphysical, and ontological.[44]

Cosmology is that theoretical discipline which attempts to frame a coherent set of categories drawn from experience which will best explain the whole. It makes use of the method of empirical generalization by which the most salient features of some paradigmatic experience are by an analogizing leap of the imagination applied to all experience. Thus, one may take as primary cosmological categories terms like "substance," "event," "feeling," "person," "monad," "complex," "process," etc. The system, coherently articulated, is testable, though never easily or simply, in terms of how well it illumines and enriches experience. Thus, for example, one might ask whether Whitehead's notion of an enduring object, a serially ordered society, adequately accounts for the continuity of intention apparently embodied in a personal act. Or again, whether Aristotle's notion of substance adequately accounts for the sense of change, novelty, and freedom which seemingly characterizes our experience in its most primordial aspect. The value in framing a cosmological hypothesis is that it provides a system of the lowest level of abstraction applicable to the whole of experience and as such it is the closest of all comprehensive and abstract systems to experience. It helps us to see the world as a whole, at least in terms of its most important features.

Another level is possible, however, and this has to do with the most general and abstract features which any determinate thing has insofar as it is determinate (and what kinds of things there are will have been decided by the cosmology chosen). It might be argued that any determinate thing must have an "inside" and an "outside" or essential and non-essential features (Weiss), possess form (Aristotle), be actual or a component of what is actual (Whitehead), or be a harmony (Neville). This is the level of metaphysics proper and implies an aprioristic or transcendental move; it asks for the necessary conditions for and the transcendental properties of any determinate thing. It is not directly suggested by experience as the cosmological categories are, nor is it either directly confirmable or falsifiable by experience.

A final level, ontology, attempts to account for the questions raised in metaphysics: why are there harmonies at all? what is the condition for the intelligibility of the world? why is there something rather than nothing? what is that in terms of which any two contingent things are related and distinguished?, etc. Obviously, the particular condition (or conditions) for the features exemplified in metaphysical analysis is (or are) relative to those features. Jung could argue both interestingly and consistently that intelligibility requires an ontological creator for the world as grasped through a cosmology which takes the individuation process as the fundamental locus of the experience of the divine. Further, this argument assumes that the question of God is not a cosmological matter at all but rather is a question raised at the metaphysical level and answerable only at the ontological. This assumes that ontology is both meaningful, possible, and necessary if anything like an intelligible and comprehensive interpretation of reality is to be attempted. Further, this argument assumes that ontology is obligatory since we ought to make our experience as rich as possible, and a good ontological theory helps us to do just that.

In light of the foregoing it would seem that Jung, having in effect denied metaphysics as he understood it as a legitimate discipline, created a cosmology of sorts, more specialized, of course, than a philosophical one, which takes the whole of experience as its subject. Jung's cosmology was broad since he took all of the Geisteswissenschaftliche concerns as his domain, omitting only what the natural sciences took as their special preserve. Any metaphysical concerns--the conditions for the possibility of knowledge, the nature and status of the archetypes per se, the transcendental properties of wholeness, etc.-- were in effect ignored as irrelevant to the "science" of psychology or included within his cosmology, albeit only incidentally. With his generally reluctant admission about God as Being Itself or transcendent being, Jung is groping toward what I have called ontology. Thus, in addition to the advantages of otherwise understanding the whole trans-empirical enterprise as a triplex of cosmology, metaphysics, and ontology, this three-fold approach helps to illuminate, nicely I think, what Jung was in fact trying to do.[45]

1
Jung to Pastor Oscar Wisse, 2 July 1960, Letters, 2:575.

2
Jung wrote to Victor White, O.P.: "God is certainly Being itself. . ." 30 June 1952, Letters, 2:73. A similar expression is to be found in his Answer to Job: "God is Reality itself. . ." (Gott das Wirkliche schlechthin ist) CW 11:402.

3
Jung to Pastor W. Niederer, 1 October 1953, Letters, 2:130.

4
Jung to Pastor Oscar Wisse, 2 July 1960, Letters, 2:575.

5
Jung to Pastor Walter Bernet, 13 June 1955, Letters, 2:259.

6
Jung to Victor White, O.P., 30 June 1952, Letters, 2:73.

7
Jung, CW 14:551.

8
Jung to Pastor Jakob Amstatz, 23 May 1955, Letters, 2:254-55.

9
Jung to Paul Maag, 12 Jung 1933, Letters, 1:125.

10
Jung speaks of the method of necessary statement by which nonarbitrary but rationally incomprehensible statements are asserted. Jung felt that the wholeness of life demanded that certain things be affirmed whether or not they were satisfactory to the intellect. See his MDR, p. 310.

11
Jung to Sir Herbert Read, 22 October 1960, Letters, 2:606.

12
Jung, CW 14:538, also CW 10:452.

13
In interpreting "the transcendent being" Jung equivocates between understanding God as creator and God as Whole, and because he also speaks of God as the unveilable mystery and as "the unfathomable itself" (see notes 8 and 9 above) he sees no need to clear up the ambiguity. He can use the traditional religious and theological language of creator and creatures, and he writes of the dependency of the subject; however, he also uses language from other traditions (idealistic, mystical, alchemical, and pantheistic)

when he speaks of God as the Whole, the One, the One
and All, the Pleroma. Note in the following how he
mixes the two languages in his lyrical amplification
of "God is love": "No language is adequate to this
paradox. Whatever one can say, no words express the
whole. To speak of partial aspects is always too much
or too little, for only the whole is meaningful...
[God is] something superior to the individual, a
unified and undivided whole. Being a part, man cannot
grasp the whole. He is at its mercy. He may assent to
it, or rebel against it; but he is always caught up by
it and enclosed within it. He is dependent upon it
and is sustained by it." (MDR, p. 354) Further, it
is clear that he understands by creation an
objectivation of God in nature; therefore, creation is
an event or temporal process within the Whole (CW
11:401). Since the Whole is a dynamic reality,
differentiating and objectifying itself, even
dialectically, comparison with Hegel is not
inappropriate. Jung admits to "a remarkable
coincidence" between some of Hegel's ideas and his own
(Jung to Joseph Rychlak, 27 April 1959, Letters,
2:502).

14

Two interesting and important features of Jung's
Letters have to be noted: (1) When first approached
about the publication of his letters, he first
selected letters to clergy (Pfarrerbriefe) for
editorial review; (2) Jung self-consciously used
letters as a means of communicating his ideas,
rectifying misinterpretations, and trying out new
ideas. Furthermore, Jung would send copies of his
letters to trusted friends for their reaction. See
editor's comments by Gerhard Adler, "Introduction,"
Letters, 1:ix. The Letters are an enormous source of
information and a resource for clarifying ideas
relatively undeveloped in the Collected Works. The
candid expression of his personal beliefs, religious
and otherwise, is quite useful and helps to
contextualize many of the points in the
Collected Works.

15

See above, Chapter One, p. 11, nn. 17-19.

16

Jung, CW 9/i:4.

17

Jung, CW 9/i:79.

18

Jung to Elisabeth Metzer, 7 February 1942,
Letters, 1:313.

19

Jung to E. L. Grant Watson, 9 February 1956, Letters, 2:289.

20

Jung to anonymous correspondent, 2 January 1957, Letters, 2:342.

21

Jung to Enrique Butelman, July 1956, Letters, 2:318.

22

Jung to Robert Dietrich, 27 March 1957, Letters, 2:355.

23

Jung to Pastor Max Frischknecht, 8 February 1946, Letters, 1:408.

24

Ibid.

25

Jung, CW 8:604 (German original); cf. also Jung to Heinrich Boltz, 13 February 1951, Letters, 2:4.

26

Jung, CW 11:5.

27

Quoted in Aniela Jaffé, The Myth of Meaning, tr. R. F. C. Hull (New York: C. G. Jung Foundation by G. P. Putnam & Sons, 1971), p. 160. According to information supplied by the translator, this letter is found in the Swiss edition only of Memories, Dreams, Reflections (p. 375).

28

Jung, CW 11:180.

29

I have drawn on the suggestive interpretation here of Richard Campbell, From Belief to Understanding (Canberra: Australian National University Press, 1976), pp. 213-222.

30

Jung, CW 11:478.

31

Jung, CW 13:49.

32

Jung to Robert C. Smith, 29 June 1960, Letters, 2:572.

33

Jung to Victor White, O.P., 5 October 1945, Letters, 1:383.

34

Most immediately this expression comes from W. H. Walsh, "Metaphysics as News from Nowhere," Metaphysics (New York: Harcourt, Brace and World, 1963), ch. 3. More remotely, the expression comes from the title of a Victorian utopian novel by William Morris.

35

Jung, CW 7:218.

36

Edward S. Casey, "Toward an Archetypal Imagination," Spring 1974: An Annual of Archetypal Psychology and Jungian Thought (New York: Spring Publications, 1974), p. 29).

37

For non-epistemological, metaphysical (or ontological) readings of Kant, See J. N. Findlay, Kant and the Transcendental Object (Oxford: Clarendon Press, 1981); Gottfried Martin, Kant's Metaphysics and Theory of Science, trans. P. G. Jucas (Manchester: The University of Manchester Press, 1955); and Martin Heidegger, Kant and the Problem of Metaphysics, trans. James S. Churchill (Bloomington: Indiana University Press, 1962).

38

Jung to Robert Dietrich, 27 March 1957, Letters, 2:355.

39

Jung to Lloyd W. Wulf. 25 July 1959, Letters, 2:512.

40

Jung CW 11:59 (modified to allow the word order of the English original--Jung wrote the essay "Psychology and Religion" in English and delivered it at the Terry Lectures at Yale University in 1937--and of the subsequent translation into German by Felicia Froboese).

41

Consider another statement written to a young theologian expressing Jung's belief in the value of his work for theology: "I always regret it when theologians take up a defensive position on the erroneous assumption that I want to put something else in the place of theology. On the contrary, I thought that theologians, in view of their apologetics, would be glad of psychological proofs which corroborate the rightness of their statements also on empirical grounds, even though this is possible only to a modest degree." Jung to Pastor Max Frischknecht, 8 February 1946, Letters, 1:412.

42

Jung, CW 12:14. Also Jung to H. Irminger, 22 September 1944, Letters, 1:350.

43

My inspiration here is Robert C. Neville, The Cosmology of Freedom (New Haven: Yale University Press, 1974), pp. 25-27.

44

Ibid.

45

Cf. a related attempt to distinguish "categorial" and "transcendental" metaphysics in Schubert Ogden, The Point of Christology (New York: Harper & Row, 1982), p. 136.

CHAPTER FIVE
THEORETICAL INTERRELATIONS

I began this essay with the claim that Jung has three theories of religious experience, not one. I have spelled out the three theories at some length, and now it is useful to compare them in order to see what relations, if any, exist among them and also to consider whether a unified theory is possible.

In the scientific-psychological theory Jung intends to explain a part of the natural world (natura), viz., psyche, which explanation is predicated upon an objective, critical inquiry-- observation, classification, hypothesis, and empirical test. In this activity a premium is put upon careful observation and inference; intuition is allowed, if at all, only as the source of hypotheses, or trial explanations. In one sense the inquirer is ideally impartial; in another as an experiencing subject the inquirer is "partial," in that only part of one's psychic functioning is deemed relevant (one's aesthetic responses, one's judgment of the value of an object, one's hunches about its future importance being scientifically beside the point). This theory is an empirical theory--empirical in the sense of observational, which is dependent upon a partial and highly specialized response by a subject to what is given. The character of this response (in addition

to the limitations which nature imposes) demarcates a
field and determines the set of possibilities for
interpretation. The subject is an inquirer; the
experienced "object" is a datum to some degree
intersubjectively observable and verifiable. The
"experience of God" is a descriptive term--it has no
explanatory value--for a datum to be interpreted
through comparison with other similar experiences with
an eye toward grasping the regularity or necessity in
the data. The datum is a quantum of psychic energy
taken as representative of the psychic system as a
whole. The libido theory provides a general
explanatory tool for understanding the regularity.

The phenomenological-mythological theory starts
with a model, an individual on a quest, different from
that of the first theory, a stream of psychic energy.
The individual searches a psychic field populated with
dynamic presences for his/her own unique wholeness.
As a phenomenological theory it emphasizes
description, a laying out of what appears, through
careful and repeated encounters with what presents
itself to the experiencer-phenomenologist. One is
particularly concerned with the symbolic imagery of
the individuation process because it is through the
involvement with such imagery that the archetypes, the
dynamic form-meanings radiating in the imagery, are
encountered. The archetypes are not postulates but
living subjects vis-à-vis the experiencer. The
subject is an engaged "becomer," a moral agent making
decisions, taking risks, and meeting challenges
inexplicably laid upon it by the dynamic powers. The
art of becoming requires one's total self, a totality
drawn forth by the numinous nature of the archetypes.

As a phenomenologist one wishes to analyze the

essence of symbols and the nature of the consciousness correlated with the various symbols. For this knowledge to be attainable one must have been or be on the path of individuation. Paradoxically, the detachment needed for knowledge and explanation requires the passionate involvement with the process of becoming. Analytical psychology as a discipline cannot be pursued fruitfully unless one is also an individuant; otherwise one would not know what to look for or how to make anything of it when found.

One notes that "psyche" has shifted from a teleologically ordered, relatively closed energy system expressible in imagery to an observing consciousness to the dynamic domain of meanings and values of person-like agencies exhibiting intentionality portrayable in symbolic imagery and events to an appropriately receptive and engaged conscious subject. Teleology is the bridge from the first to the second meanings of "psyche" and from the scientific to the phenomenological theories. As in the former theory the "experience of God" describes an experience of something in the psychic domain, but the "something" is not so much a question of energy as a dynamic agent with power to heal and transform. The archetypes explain the God-imagery and the experience of numinosity. Yet the very nature of their activity requires a more practical rather than a more theoretical explanation--the decisions of personal agents rather than the movements of abstract energy.

There is a sense in which a phenomenological-mythological theory is more primordial, more foundational than the scientific-psychological theory. The abstractions of science presuppose the intentions of persons, and not conversely. This does not mean, however, that the scientific theory does not attempt to formalize the noetic elements of which even a decision must take note. In another sense the model on which the scientific-psychological theory is based--the stream model--is a necessary condition for the possibility for the quest model; personal decision presupposes life. The interrelation between the two "empirical" theories is dialectical; without the phenomenological the scientific would be meaningless, and yet without the scientific the phenomenological would lack the distantiation of subject from object needed for a comprehension of experience, especially experience involving personal agents.

While both theories focus in different ways on the world of experience, each providing an important element in the total explanation, their restriction to what is given in experience, largely sensory, is felt to be a limitation if understanding is to be adequate to experience. Human beings seem to need to hook their experiences into larger frameworks of meaning; the experience of numinosity naturally suggests an ontological grounding; archetypes are sensed as forms normative for wide reaches of experience; the healing of human personality suggests the trans-human, not simply trans-individual elements in the human. Moreover, neither of the first two theories can account for the sense of creatureliness, of dependency and submission, which Jung admits as important features of experience.[1] Furthermore, the experience of utter mystery, of "numinous inconceivability,"[2] suggests in some sense an Anselmian "that than which none greater can be conceived." The hypothesizing of God as an explanatory principle, and not simply as a descriptive term for immanental cosmic features, seems

necessary for full comprehension of experience. The
criterion of adequacy to experience pushes for an
explanatory principle beyond experience.

The metaphysical-theological theory of religious
experience attempts to explain the empirical dimension
not of observation nor even of the dialectics of lived
experience but of existence. In some sense the
observables and experienceables are concrete
existents, crying out for some explanation adequate to
the fact that they are, to the fact that they exist
dependently and contingently. Existence, at least as
humans sense it, evokes acknowledgement and
confession, and there must be some explanation for
this fact. Explanation of the "full fact" sooner or
later must include the ontological else the empirical
is left improperly grasped. Paradoxically, if there
is no good metaphysical-theological theory, the
concrete cannot even be fully experienced as concrete.
Metaphysics provides an enormous practical service.

It might be asked whether or not Jung's three
theories, once having been explicated and once having
their interrelations worked out, might not be combined
into a single comprehensive theory. Jung's thought,
so it might be argued, would, at least on the issue of
religious experience, be a unified whole. This, I
argue, is neither possible nor desirable.

It is impossible, first of all, because the
theories have different levels of conceptual scope.
Theories by their nature are field-referential; to
change the scope of the field is to change what needs
an explanation (explanandum) and what can do the
explaining (explanans). Furthermore, the demand for a
single theory ignores the conceptually different
activities involved in science, phenomenology, and

metaphysics. To treat science as if it were phenomenology, and conversely, is to distort both. With the necessary demand for conceptual clarity and precision science cannot adequately deal with the pre-thematic, ambiguous, axiological, and ontological aspects of experience. With the necessary demand for attentiveness to the pre-thematic aspects of lived-experience, phenomenology, at least of the sort that is applicable to the human world, cannot adequately deal with the abstractions of energy systems and their movements or of the universal categories of cosmology and the ultimate metaphysical ground. Even if it were possible, it would not be desirable in that the potential increase in the richness of experience, which responsible theorizing engenders, would be diminished. The richest degree of experiential contrast is the goal of existence. To view the world only under the umbrella of science is to see precisely but not importantly enough. To view the world only under the umbrella of phenomenology is to see importantly but not comprehensively enough. To view the world metaphysically is to see comprehensively and to see importantly but to see only vaguely (i.e., non-specifically). The goal is to see precisely and importantly and comprehensively. At least three different kinds of theories are needed.

At their best, different kinds of theories provide external checks and tests on and for each other. A metaphysical hypothesis has to be specified in such a way that at least some empirical findings could count toward confirmation, if not disconfirmation, of the theory. Here both scientific and phenomenological results, legitimized by their respective theories, can serve as the necessary empirical test of a metaphysical hypothesis. A metaphysical hypothesis can provide a theoretical framework in which concepts of lesser scope can be interpreted and rival hypotheses evaluated.

Yet surely it is misplaced concreteness to take a metaphysical theory as a specific explanation of what is experienced. To lack scientific-psychological and phenomenological-mythological explanation is to lack all mediating and specifying structures between concrete fact and abstract understanding. Without mediating structures there is no responsible theorizing since experience could be interpreted by any general theory. Metaphysics by itself leads to a removal from the world of experience, which is an impoverishment of experience and a distortion of metaphysics. Metaphysics is not the re-creation of experience but the explanation of such.[3] Certainly some hypothesizing close to the lived-world of value, purpose, meaning, and intention helps the experiencer to see nuances in the concrete fact and prevent what Quine somewhere calls an "excess of notation over meaning," a particularly pernicious tendency of the abstracting intellect. Some hypothesizing which redescribes a personal world in terms of structures, relations, and energy patterns prevents an over-lushness of immediacy; and by presenting an alternative explanation to the most abstract systems it prevents the swallowing up of concrete experience, which would mean the stultification of life. The proper understanding of the world, including religious experience, requires a dialectical relationship among theories of different levels of abstractness and scope.

Jung's three theories provide one model of how religious experience requires for the fullest understanding a differentiated theoretical approach. Difficulties can be found with each of the three theories, and I have done so; yet something like a threefold approach is required as exemplified in Jung's work.

[1]
Jung, MDR, p. 354.

[2]
Jung to Lloyd W. Wolf,25 July 1959, <u>Letters</u>, 2:512.

[3]
Here and elsewhere I am deeply indebted to Robert C. Neville's writings for my understanding of metaphysics, explanation, and the relation of metaphysics to experience. Since metaphysics ultimately intends to explain what is important in experience, these three notions cannot be treated in isolation from each other. Relevant passages are <u>God the Creator</u> (Chicago: University of Chicago Press, 1968), Part Two; <u>The Cosmology of Freedom</u> (New Haven: Yale University Press, 1974), Chapter 2; <u>Soldier, Sage, Saint</u> (New York: Fordham University Press, 1978), Chapter 5; <u>Creativity and God</u> (New York: Seabury Press, 1980), Chapter 4; <u>The Tao and the Daimon</u> (Albany: State University of New York Press, 1982), Chapters 1-4, 6, and 7; "Specialties and Worlds," <u>Hastings Center Studies</u> 2(January 1974):53-64; "Metaphysics," <u>Social Research</u> 47(Winter 1980):686-703.

SELECTED BIBLIOGRAPHY

Works by Jung

The Collected Works of C. G. Jung. Editors: Sir Herbert Read, Michael Fordham, Gerhard Adler; William McGuire, executive editor. Translated by R. F. C. Hull (except vol. 6). Bollingen Series 20.

Vol. 4: Freud and Psychoanalysis. Princeton: Princeton University Press, 1961.

Vol. 5: Symbols of Transformation: An Analysis of the Prelude to a Case of Schizophrenia. 2nd ed. Princeton: Princeton University Press, 1967.

Vol. 6: Psychological Types. A revision by R. F. C. Hull of the translation of H. G. Baynes. Princeton: Princeton University Press, 1971.

Vol. 7: Two Essays on Analytical Psychology. 2nd ed. Princeton: Princeton University Press, 1972.

Vol. 8: The Structure and Dynamics of the Psyche. 2nd ed. Princeton: Princeton University Press, 1969.

Vol. 9, Part 1: The Archetypes and the Collective Unconscious. 2nd ed. Princeton: Princeton University Press, 1969.

Vol. 9, Part 2: Aion: Researches into the Phenomenology of the Self. 2nd ed. Princeton: Princeton University Press, 1968.

Vol. 10: <u>Civilization in Transition</u>. 2nd ed. Princeton: Princeton University Press, 1970.

Vol. 11: <u>Psychology and Religion: West and East</u>. 2nd ed. Princeton: Princeton University Press, 1968.

Vol. 12: <u>Psychology and Alchemy</u>. 2nd ed. Princeton: Princeton University Press, 1967.

Vol. 13: <u>Alchemical Studies</u>. Princeton: Princeton University Press, 1967.

Vol. 17: <u>The Development of Personality</u>. New York: Bollingen Foundation, 1964.

Vol. 18: <u>The Symbolic Life</u>. Princeton: Princeton University Press, 1976.

<u>Briefe</u>. Edited by Aniela Jaffe and Gerhard Adler. 3 vols. Olten, Switzerland: Walter-Verlag, 1973. Vol. 3.

<u>C. G. Jung: Letters</u>. Edited by Gerhard Adler and Aniela Jaffe. Translated by R. F. C. Hull. Bollingen Series 95:1. 2 vols. Princeton: Princeton University Press, 1973-1975.

<u>Die Dynamik des Unbewussten</u>. Vol. 8 of <u>Gesammelte Werke</u>. Olten und Freiburg im Breisgau: Walter-Verlag, 1971.

<u>Memories, Dreams, Reflections</u>. Edited by Aniela Jaffe and translated by Richard and Clara Winston. New York: Vintage Books, 1963

<u>Psychology of the Unconscious</u>. Translated by B. M. Hinckle. New York: Dodd, Mead & Co., 1965.

<u>The Visions Seminars</u>. 2 vols. New York: Spring Publications, 1976. Vol. 2.

<u>Zur Psychologie westlicher und ostlicher Religion</u>. Vol. 11 of <u>Gesammelte Werke</u>. Zurich: Rascher Verlag, 1963.

<u>Works about Jung</u>

Baumann, Carol. "Psychological Experiences Connected with Childbirth." In <u>Studien zur analytischen</u>

psychologie C. G. Jungs. Zurich: Rascher & Cie., 1955.

Brent, T. David. "Jung's Debt to Kant: The Transcendental Method and the Structure of Jung's Psychology." Ph.D. dissertation, University of Chicago, 1977.

Ellenberger, Henri F. The Discovery of the Unconscious: The History and Evolution of Dynamic Psychiatry. New York: Basic Books, 1970.

Glover, Edward. Freud or Jung? New York: World Publishing Company, 1965.

Goldenberg, Naomi R. "Jung After Feminism." In Beyond Androcentrism, pp. 53-66. Edited by Rita M. Gross. Missoula, Montana: Scholars Press, 1977.

Gunter, P. A. Y. "Bergson and Jung." Journal of the History of Ideas 43(October-December 1982):635-652.

Hall, Calvin S. and Nordby, Vernon J. A Primer of Jungian Psychology. New York: New American Library, 1973.

Heisig, James W. Imago Dei: A Study of C. G. Jung's Psychology of Religion. Lewisburg, Pennsylvania: Bucknell University Press, 1979.

Homans, Peter. Jung in Context. Chicago: University of Chicago Press, 1979.

Hostie, Raymond. Religion and the Psychology of C. G. Jung. Translated by G. R. Lamb. New York: Sheed & Ward, 1957.

Hoy, Daniel J. "Numinous Experiences: Frequent or Rare?" Journal of Analytical Psychology 28(January 1983):17-32.

Jacobi, Jolande. Complex/Archetype/Symbol. Translated by Ralph Manheim. Bollingen Series 57. New York: Pantheon Books, 1959.

_____. The Psychology of C. G. Jung. Translated by Ralph Manheim. New Haven: Yale University Press, 1976.

Jaffé, Aniela. The Myth of Meaning. Translated by R.
    F. C. Hull. New York: C. G. Jung Foundation by
    G. P. Putnam & Sons, 1971.

McGuire, William, and Hull, R. F. C., eds. C. G. Jung
    Speaking. Bollingen Series 97. Princeton:
    Princeton University Press, 1977.

Progoff, Ira. Jung's Psychology and its Social
    Meaning. 2nd ed. New York: Julian Press, 1969.

Singer, June. Boundaries of the Soul. Garden City,
    New York: Doubleday & Co., 1972.

Uchizono, Roy. "Science and Metaphysics in the
    Psychology of C. G. Jung: An Interpretation."
    Ph.D. dissertation, Claremont Graduate School and
    University Center, 1964.

von Franz, Marie-Louise. C. G. Jung: His Myth in Our
    Time. Translated by William H. Kennedy. New
    York: C. G. Jung Foundation, 1975.

Wolff, Toni. Studien zu C. G. Jungs Psychologie.
    Zurich: Rhein-Verlag, 1959.

Other

Barbour, Ian. Myths, Models, and Paradigms. New
    York: Harper & Row, 1974.

Campbell, Richard. From Belief to Understanding.
    Canberra: Australian National University Press,
    1976.

Casey, Edward S. "Toward an Archetypal Imagination."
    In Spring: An Annual of Archetypal Psychology and
    Jungian Thought (1974):1-32.

Farley, Edward. Ecclesial Man. Philadelphia: Fortress
    Press, 1975.

Findlay, J. N. Kant and the Transcendental Object.
    Oxford: Clarendon Press, 1981.

Heidegger, Martin. Kant and the Problem of
    Metaphysics. Translated by James. S. Churchill.
    Bloomington: Indiana University Press, 1962.

Lauer, Quentin. Phenomenology: Its Genesis and
    Prospect. New York: Harper & Row, 1965.

Malinowski, Bronislaw. Magic, Science and Religion.
    Edited by Robert Redfield. Garden City, New
    York: Doubleday & Co., 1955.

McCain, Garvin and Segal, Erwin M. The Game of
    Science. 3rd ed. Monterey, California:
    Brooks/Cole Publishing Co., 1977.

Martin, Gottfried. Kant's Metaphysics and Theory of
    Science. Translated by P. G. Lucas. Manchester:
    University of Manchester Press, 1955.

Neville, Robert C. The Cosmology of Freedom. New
    Haven: Yale University Press, 1974.

------. Creativity and God. New York: Seabury Press,
    1980.

_____. God the Creator. Chicago: University of
    Chicago Press, 1968.

_____. "Metaphysics." Social Research 47(Winter
    1980):686-703.

_____. Soldier, Sage, Saint. New York: Fordham University Press, 1978.

_____. "Specialties and Worlds." Hastings Center Studies 2(January,1974):53-64.

_____. The Tao and The Daimon. Albany: State University of New York Press, 1982.

Nietzsche, Friedrich. Thus Spake Zarathustra. In The Portable Nietzsche. Edited and translated by Walter Kaufmann. New York: Viking Press, 1954.

Ogden, Schubert. The Point of Christology. New York: Harper & Row, 1982.

Otto, Rudolf. The Idea of the Holy. Translated by John W. Harvey. 2nd ed. London: Oxford University Press, 1958.

Pauck, Wilhelm, and Pauck, Marion. Paul Tillich: His Life and Thought. Vol. 1: Life. New York: Harper & Row, 1976.

Ricoeur, Paul. Husserl: An Analysis of His Phenomenology. Translated by Edward G. Ballard and Lester E. Embree, Evanston: Northwestern University Press, 1967.

_____. Interpretation Theory. Fort Worth: Texas Christian University Press, 1976.

_____. The Symbolism of Evil. Translated by Emerson Buchanan. New York: Harper & Row, 1967.

Smith, Huston. Forgotten Truth. New York: Harper & Row, 1976.

Smith, John E. Experience and God. New York: Oxford University Press, 1968.

Snyder, Paul. Toward One Science. New York: St. Martin's Press, 1978.

Spiegelberg, Herbert. Phenomenology in Psychology and Psychiatry. Evanston: Northwestern University Press, 1972.

_____. The Phenomenological Movement: A Historical Introduction. 2nd. ed. 2 vols. The Hague: Martinus Nijhoff, 1965. Vol. 1.

Walsh, W. H. Metaphysics. New York: Harcourt, Brace & World, 1963.

Whitehead, Alfred North. Process and Reality. New York: Macmillan & Co., 1929.

Zaner, Richard M. The Way of Phenomenology. New York: Western Publishing Company, 1970.

INDEX

A priori concepts and knowledge, 37-38, 105, 128
Actuality, 144
Adler, Alfred, 39
Adults: psychic development, 27-28
Age and youth, 84
Alchemists, 128
Alchemy, 81, 84
Alienation, 79
Amazon(image), 73
Ambiguity, 104
Ambiguity in Jung's language, 131-133
Ambivalence, 25, 95
Analogy, 28, 44, 45
Analytical psychology, 91
Androgyny/androgynous, 89
Animal psyche, 26-27
Animals, 31
Appresentation, 102-107
Apperception: defined, 103; analogy vs. intuition, 104; background realities, 105-106; and intuition, 109
Archetypal image of the Deity, 141, 142
Archetype(s): appearance in literature, 35; attributes of the creator, 126, 127; availability, 118 n.54; characteristics, 128; confusion of usage, 115n.25; "consciousness," 98; danger of, 136; defined, 4-5; description, 48; direct encounter with God, 125; effect on subject, 110; explanation and disclosure (of functions), 130-131; and givenness, 100-102; how experienced, 110, 111; irrepresentability of, 129; as metaphysical, 130, 138; model, 74-75; as numina, 94-95; numinous (usage), 124-127; and numinosity, 12, 89, 90; objective psyche, 90; per se, 75; perception, 99; and psychic energy, 22; rhetoric, 128-129; source of

term, 128; and spirit, 85; status, 98-102; as structural elements of life, 47; as "tools of God," 124-125; transgressivity, 139; usage in "On the Nature of the Psyche," 52n.4
Aristotle; form, 144; horme, 43; and individuation, 81; substance, 144
Art, 84
Attitude, 38-39
Augustine, Saint, 128
Autonomy, 26-27, 83
Autonomy, moral, 20

Background, 7, 90, 109
Background realities, 105-106
Barbour, Ian 40
Barth, Karl, 141
Being Itself. See God
Belief, 15, 54n.8, 96, 97
Bergson, Henri, 43, 82
Binswanger, Ludwig, 113n.7
Bivalence, 89
Bleuler, Eugen, 118n.51
Body language, 56n.31
Bonhoeffer, Dietrich, 96
Boss, Medard, 113n.7
Boundless, 94
Buber, Martin 134-135
Buddha, 31
Bultmann, Rudolf Karl, 141
Burckhardt, Jakob, 72

Casey, Edward, 137
Cause and effect, 17
Charybdis, 136
Childbirth, 74
Children, 19, 27
Christ, Jesus. See Jesus Christ
Christ, love of, 27
Christian Cross, 84
Christianity: and love, 34; and numinous, 94; religionless, 96; role in evolution, 26; role in psychic economy, 56 n.34; and sexual repression, 30, 33

Studies in the Psychology of Religion